Glossary of Terms

4MP *n.* abbreviation for The Four Man Plan

4MPlanner *n.* a woman who is practicing The Four Man Plan

Chick's Chick *n.* a woman who honors all women and their relationships

Chuck *v.* to remove a Two and a Quarter Man from The Four Man Plan because his 4MPlanner is sleeping with someone new

Dick's Chick *n.* a woman who throws herself at married or otherwise monogamous men

Half Man *n.* a Plan Man whom a 4MPlanner has had at least three dates with and/or knows that she is seeing other men

Mantris Graph *n.* a square 4 × 4 grid used by a 4MPlanner to track the progress of her Plan Men

postulate *n.* something that is assumed to be true and that is used as the basis of an argument or theory

principle *n.* an accepted or professed rule of action or conduct

Prince Charming *n.* a mythical creature whose debunking leads to trauma and drama

Plan Man *n.* any man who is dating a 4MPlanner

Quarter Man *n.* a Plan Man who has had contact but no more than two dates with a 4MPlanner

theory *n.* a coherent group of general propositions used to explain a class of phenomena

Three and a Half Man *n.* the Plan Man who can be described as honest, loving, and willing and has initiated and been accepted into a monogamous relationship with a 4MPlanner

Two and a Quarter Man *n.* the one Plan Man whom a 4MPlanner is sleeping with

Whole Man *n.* 1. a Plan Man who has spoken the word "love" to his 4MPlanner 2. a Plan Man who has gotten to second base with his 4MPlanner

BROADWAY BOOKS   New York

THE
FOUR MAN
PLAN

A Romantic Science

Cindy Lu

PUBLISHED BY BROADWAY BOOKS

Copyright © 2007 by Cindy Lu

All Rights Reserved

Published in the United States by Broadway Books, an imprint of
The Doubleday Broadway Publishing Group, a division of
Random House, Inc., New York.

www.broadwaybooks.com

BROADWAY BOOKS and its logo, a letter B bisected on the diagonal,
are trademarks of Random House, Inc.

For illustration credits, see page 211.

Library of Congress Cataloging-in-Publication Data

Lu, Cindy.
The Four man plan : a romantic science / Cindy Lu. — 1st ed.
p. cm.
1. Man-woman relationships—United States—Anecdotes.
2. Dating (Social customs)—United States—Anecdotes.
I. Title. II. Title: 4 man plan.

HQ801.L79 2007
306.730973—dc22

2007019229

ISBN 978-0-7679-2857-1

PRINTED IN THE UNITED STATES OF AMERICA

1 3 5 7 9 10 8 6 4 2

First Edition

For Earl, my husband, my Three and a Half Man

Contents

ARE YOU FABULOUS AND SINGLE?
VERY, VERY SINGLE?

Try This . . .

The 4MP*

"The search for truth is more precious than its possession."
—ALBERT EINSTEIN

*Abbreviation of The Four Man Plan. Also referred to as The Plan.

4word

In July 2006, a one-woman show, *The Four Man Plan,* premiered in a tiny theater with a stack of self-published books on sale in the lobby. To be honest, when I called it a Dating Revolution at that time, I really thought it could be, but I was kind of blowing smoke. Turns out, I'm superpsychic! It's all that and a box of bonbons. It's not only a Dating Revolution, to all us girls The 4MP is Dating's *Evolution.* It is an easy-to-follow scientific system that will teach you the basics of love, internal and external, as it should have been taught around the same time as high school.

The only requirement to becoming a 4MPlanner is a desire to take charge of your love life. Not just wishing and hoping and gluing pictures of J. Crew male models onto your vision board, I mean getting down and dirty with the subject of love and doing something about getting more of it into your life.

To my giddy delight and surprise, The 4MP is now being experimented with and enjoyed by everyone from teenage girls to sexagenarians. And just recently, I received news of a 4MPlanner getting *engaged* just five months after starting The Plan. They are blogging and cataloging, laughing and graphing all the way to the altar!

The input I've received from real women trying The Plan, whether loyalists or dabblers, has been invaluable. In this edition, I wanted to answer their questions and include their insights. The Four Man Plan is, after all, about what we can do to help one another and love ourselves.

If someone has given you this book as a gift, one of three things is happening:

1. Your gal pal is a 4MPlanner and having a blast. It's definitely more fun with your friends along for the ride. Join in!

2. Your friend / relative / coworker is pretty sure you suck at love and is looking to give you a leg up. Don't be offended—they love you and want you to be happy.

3. Your parents are using this book to replace or augment the awkward parent / child "sex talk." Trust me, you'll get the straight poop here from your cool aunt Cindy. Feel free to discuss it with them after you've read it. (It's probably what they are hoping for.)

Are You Ready?

The structure for dating, the clear-cut answers about relationships that you've been waiting for, is finally here! The Four Man Plan starts where therapy and self-help books leave off. To begin, let us assume that you recognize that your parents are somewhere between flawed and psychotic, and that whatever was messing them up has had its part in messing you up. Cop to it and don't let it get you down. It is not a life sentence.

It is a given that you have put considerable effort into the love thing and you are now in the red. All the time, energy, sacrifice, and heartache you have invested has added up to nothing more than a pile of empty Kleenex boxes, some blocked phone numbers, and one too many goddess ceremonies.

It is taken for granted that you are fabulous, smart, well liked, and successful in most other areas of your life. You have used your single time wisely to pursue your friendships and your career and your personal development. You're independent; you know you don't *need* a man. You are not a loser, you're just single. Maybe it's because you're dating aimlessly. Maybe you're in love with someone who just won't give you what you need. Or maybe you're dreading-Valentine's-Day, cooking-for-one, sleeping-with-your-cat single. Very, very single. Are you starting to suspect that love is not your best subject?

In my circle of very smart and savvy single girlfriends, we swapped several forms of co-misery on a regular basis:

a. **Bizarre dating stories:**
   "My date had five martinis in one hour."
   "My date had six toes on one foot."

b. **Frantic pleas for advice:**
   "Am I allowed to break up via e-mail?"
   "What does it mean when he gives you a key and then changes the locks?"

c. **Deep contemplations on a man-less existence:**
   "Is lesbianism something that can be learned?"
   "Where do I pick up a nun application?"

d. Sweeping declarations against men:

"Snowball and I are doing just fine on our own!"

"A handyman and a vibrating 'neck massager' is all I need!"

For today's women, these sentiments are common. We don't know how to get the responses we crave from men. Either a sense of desperation and competition lights our panties on fire, or hopelessness and snap judgments turn our bedrooms into icy tundras. Finding ourselves in a healthy, mutual relationship with a man who is honest, loving, and willing seems as unlikely as the whole toad-turning-into-a-prince line of BS we were fed as impressionable young girls. And as a result, women as a gender have been set askew.

Let's face it, we know there is no jolly fat guy in a red suit. We know there is no giant bunny with a basket of painted eggs. We know there is no molar-obsessed fairy with a wing-ful of five-dollar bills. So why the hell would we still believe that there is some perfectly chiseled, castle-owning hottie who looks great in tights searching for us so he can fulfill his lifelong dream of sweeping us off our feet? Believing that your future love is *"out there somewhere and will find me some-day!"* is about as practical as believing that about your lunch or your next paycheck.

While trying to pursue the elusive Prince Charming, I sold myself short, behaved badly, and put up with being disrespected over and over again. It took up a lot of my time and energy and left me feeling lonely and jaded. The Four Man Plan was my formula for setting myself straight.

Why do I need a plan?

Making a plan is not an act of desperation. It is the ultimate expression of faith and optimism. A plan simply outlines a design whose completion will still require divine input, surprise assistance, and all the other good stuff that makes life fun. It channels your efforts and articulates the intent that your desires are meant to be brought to life. Making a plan and sticking to it helps you weather the inevitable ups and downs that are inherent in obtaining anything worthwhile.

How effective is The Four Man Plan? I was about nine months into doing The 4MP when a handsome, successful, faithful, and sweet surprise of a man captured my heart. We have been together for over six years and live in a cute house with our three dogs. On March 10, 2007, we were married. It's taken a lot of work to get here, but we are happy, stable, and in love. That's right, I am the first success story of The Four Man Plan!

The following are reasonable expectations for any gal who gives The 4MP a college try:

- Raise your self-esteem by placing a higher value on yourself, your energy, your heart, and your vagina.

- Choose and encourage men of quality and honor.

- Become the *selector,* not the *selectee.*

- Find emotional balance.

- Update a long-malfunctioning system of love.

- Make single life way more fun.

All that being said, going the extra mile and nerding out on The Plan may earn you the highest grade of all:

ONE man to save your seat, rub your feet, and grill your meat into happily ever after.

Will it work for you? You do the math.

(Don't worry, you don't have to actually be good at math. I'll help you every step of the way.)

If You Are a Man

One of three things is going on:

1. **You've accidentally stumbled into the ladies' room.**
   Exit quietly, no one noticed.
2. **You are a genius.**
   You know a 4MPlanner and you realized that the playbook was available to you. There is no harm or foul in your knowing and comprehending The Plan. There is a wealth of information for you that will help you get ahead with your girl, and she should appreciate that you have taken the time to do your homework.
3. **You are a gay man.**
   Oh goodie! I'm currently gathering data on gay men and The Plan. I need your input! Try it and then pretty please e-mail me and let me know how it works for you guys! www.thefourmanplan.com.

1. THE FUNDAMENTAL EQUATION

$$4 \, (m)^P = u + 1$$

Four times men, to the power of The Plan, becomes you plus another.

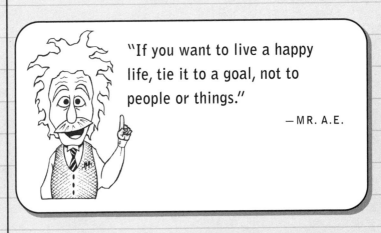

"If you want to live a happy life, tie it to a goal, not to people or things."

— MR. A.E.

Enter the equation . . .

Lu's Fundamental Equation for Finding Love

Okay, hang with this for a second.

In science, a **fundamental equation** is an equation that expresses physical law. For example, the most famous is Einstein's fundamental equation for relativity:

$$E = mc^2$$

$E = mc^2$ is the equation that expresses *an equivalence between energy (E) and mass (m), in direct proportion to the square of the speed of light in a vacuum (c²).* Basically, Einstein is saying that "energy and mass are two forms of the same thing."

All the cool scientist kids have their own fundamental equations, so this is mine:

$$4(m)^p = u + 1$$

This equation expresses the physical law that *four times the men (m), to the power of The Plan (p), becomes you (u) and another (+ 1).* Basically, I'm saying "get off your butt, try something new, and stop whining, and you'll end up with a permanent date."

Let's break it down.

$4{(m)}^p$

Four Times Men to the Power of The Plan = The Rebirth of Chivalry

Do you ever wonder why there are so many *boys* and so few *men* out there? It's because something really yucky is being propagated in our current culture. We seem to be accepting the notion that being slutty is cool. The evidence of this is the large number of girls willing to flash their tits and pretend to be lesbians for a pitcher of margaritas and a dram of nameless attention.

Some women have also been misled to believe that the path to love and success is paved with the broken spirits of other women because there just aren't enough good men to go around. What we don't recognize is that every man can become a good man.

You may find this hard to believe, but given the right opportunities and environment, chivalry comes naturally to men. Activating their competitive instinct during the pursuit of love simultaneously activates their desire to be chivalrous. Chivalry has been waning steadily in our culture, because when women compete with each other and start doling out blow jobs like hand shakes, it gives men very little to strive for. The Four Man is the Petrie Dish of Gallantry.

There is only so much they can learn from Mommy. We all know that guy who is a sweetheart to his mother and a cad to the women he dates. It is up to us, their partner-potential females, to show them the natural way to treat *all* women, which is with deep respect for the gorgeous, enigmatic, beguiling creatures that we were designed to be.

If women decide *as a gender* that we deserve to be treated with honor and respect, then men will react accordingly and rise up *as a gender* to meet our requirements.

We can create the hybrid Steinem/Guinevere generation, where we retain every bit of our equality and social progress while reasserting our right to be treated like princesses. Let's make them earn it, girls.

$$P = U$$

The Power of The Plan Becomes You

There are two translations for this statement:

1. The Four Man Plan is designed to help you become more yourself. One of the fundamentals you learn while you are dating multiple men is that it's not all about them. The Plan is about you, your ability to love yourself and be treated well.

2. The Four Man Plan looks great on a woman.

$u + 1$

You and Another

U + 1 means the most fabulous you, *plus* ONE WORTHY MAN who is your true partner, best friend, and smokin' lover.

Let me state for the record that there is nothing wrong with being single. Sometimes it's exactly where you need to be. Without my outrageously fun, uninhibited, and enlightening singlehood, I would not be the amazingly cool chick I am today. But there comes a time in your life when your name gets put on a guest list as You Plus One; you just want to know for certain who the frig that person is, all the time.

Having a clear goal line, you plus one, can keep you going when The Plan gets tough. It is designed to prepare you for love and invite a man of quality into your life. But a good thing to keep in mind is that no one man is responsible for your happiness. That is a solo project. The happier you are with yourself, the better the partner you will be adding to your life.

"If you want to live a happy life, tie it to a goal, not to people or things."

–ALBERT EINSTEIN

LEGEND OF THE 4MP

YES, you will be dating up to a total of four Whole Men at the same time. But all men are not created equal. Each man in your plan, or "Plan Man," qualifies for one of four basic values.

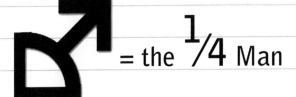 = the $\frac{1}{4}$ Man

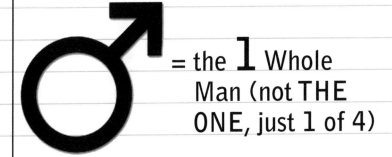 = the $\frac{1}{2}$ Man

= the 1 Whole Man (not THE ONE, just 1 of 4)

THE 2¼ MAN

Fear not, sex is part of The 4MP.

This is not some thinly veiled Sunday-school reader.

More details to come . . .

2. THE BACK STORY

Disclosure of the events that led to the
creation of The 4MP.

"Insanity: doing the same
thing over and over again and
expecting different results."

— AL

A Complex Cinderella

One of my therapists, and oh I've had many, told me that five is the age that little girls romanticize their fathers. That explains A LOT.

When I was five, my mom and dad divorced, and it was ugly. No, seriously, really, really ugly. Witnessing their marriage and its demise was pretty much all it took to completely screw me up.

I spent approximately the next twenty-five years obsessing over the wrong men and cultivating a disastrous love life. Three things drove me to my doom: a Cinderella fantasy, a defiance against the rantings of a scorned mother, and an unscratchable love itch left by the sting of an abandoning father.

Right before they split for good and soon after I started school in America, in a diplomatic effort to unite them through parental pride, I convinced my parents to attend an assembly in which I was to be named the Student of the Month. Being the new girl had been tough and my Chinese given name, An-Pai, had become An-Peepee and An-Poopoo in the hands of my fellow kindergartners. But this was my chance to shine. My proud moment was dashed, however, when my teacher mispronounced my name "An-Pie" and a boy from my class yelled out, "Ann PIE FACE!" and the room erupted. I swear I even saw the principal snicker.

Here's what made me fall in love with my father: The next day, he came home with school forms and asked my sister and me to choose new, American names. My sister chose

"Linda" because she had recently learned that it meant "beautiful" in Spanish. Predisposed to competing with her for the crumbs of love my father doled out, I chose *"Cinderella! The most beautiful girl in the whole world!"*

Hey, I was five. Admit it, you would have, too.

He shortened it to Cindy. I'd like to think it was an act of mercy, but it was probably an inability to spell Cinderella and the inherent Chinese aversion to all those *r*s and *l*s. My fantasy name would become my longest-held secret and Cinderella's happily ever after would become my longest-held dream.

What I knew about my father at that age was that he was a sixth-degree black belt who could move so fast he was blurry when I watched him. He was handsome and tall and could produce lightning bolts of healing energy with his hands. He was cool and talented and hung out with famous people like Muhammad Ali and the L.A. Rams.

What I didn't know then was that he gambled, he loved danger, and he had wanted sons. Soon after he dubbed me the Cindy of Cinderellas, he ditched our family for a China Airlines flight attendant half his age.

My mother was left alone in a foreign country to fend for herself and her two daughters, with no English and no job skills. She was *pissed*. And that's when my mom renamed him. Some of her first American words were **"Liar! Cheater! Son of a Bitch!"** Who could blame her? Cursing him and all men became a daily ritual. But I loved him, missed him, and wanted to be with *him,* not her.

Unconsciously, those events set me on a quest to prove

my mother wrong about men and to succeed where she had failed. My goal:

The Daddy Redemption Quest

Objective #1. Find a man like my father (i.e., a liar, a cheater, a player, and an emotionally detached dreamer who didn't know I was alive).

Objective #2. Make him fall in love with me.

Objective #3. Change him into a loyal, loving man and **make him stay with me forever.**

To me, nothing was hotter than the back of a man's head as he was walking out the door.

A Mess o' Exes

During my adolescence, a day did not go by that I didn't take some time to obsess about my love life. Or, more honestly, my internal dialogue about my most current target guy would be occasionally interrupted by other thoughts. I could have been a clinical study for the disease that is so flippantly called "Boy Crazy." I remember having a crush on my teacher in first grade, and by the third grade I was chasing boys around at recess trying to kiss them. I used to daydream about hanging out backstage with Keith Partridge, riding around on Ponch's motorcycle, and punching out Joanie to get to Chachi. As soon as I was old enough to date, I couldn't wait to turn fantasy into reality, quest into conquest.

At age eighteen, I landed my first boyfriend, Johnny. He was an awesome surfer with a high-school-sweetheart girl-friend back home in Detroit. But whatever, she was too far away for either of us to give a damn about *her* feelings. He just liked to bring her up now and then to let me know that there was someone out there whom he *really* loved. He gave me my first orgasm and swiftly followed it with my first bong hit; "Surfer Speedball" he called it. How could I *not* fall in love with the guy? But he considered the ocean "his West Coast girl," and he was always leaving me for her even though she routinely beat the crap out of him. Making me *third* on his list.

Next was Anthony, a Shakespearean actor twice my age. He took me under his wing and explained to me that it was very important to his craft to "get to know," which meant at least make out with, ALL his leading ladies. That led to a very "open" relationship, which can get a little awkward when you're sharing a one-bedroom apartment. The last I saw of him was as Oberon, driving off with a newly cast Titania and a car full of fairies.

Stephan was an ice sculptor with an unidentifiable Britishy accent. How cool is that? He loved for me to sit on the block of ice he was carving up in the walk-in freezer. He'd wield a chain saw and a chisel, a cigarette dangling from his lip, wearing only a tank top, jeans, and big black rubber boots. He would get bleary-eyed on absinthe and call me his muse while rejected ice chunks and mangled snow flew up around me. He was a selfish lover but was only mean to me while he was sleepwalking. Just when I had made my list of things I was going to change about him, he disappeared after somehow setting fire to a country club's linen closet. How weird is that?

Creepy Eddie was a long-distance romance, and he was only sixteen years older than me. He was successful and rich and said he loved me on the pornographic audiotapes he liked to send me. On one of my visits, he rented the 1944 classic *Gaslight* because he couldn't believe I hadn't seen his favorite movie! Long after we agreed to be monogamous, he told me that the empty condom wrapper I had found under our bed was used while he masturbated to "cut down on the mess." He even had his best friend confess to doing the same. This same friend confirmed Eddie's ridiculously lame excuse for an overnight disappearance where he returned smelling of artificial peaches and sporting a new hairdo. The truth was that he had been banging his ankleless hairdresser, Gilda. According to the love letters I found in his file cabinet that same week (yes, I was snooping), I thought he had been fucking his neighbor! Turns out, it was both. And those were only the ones I found evidence for. He executed several successful bids to make me feel like I was crazy and that my shady methods of acquiring evidence made my case inadmissible. I finally realized that Charles Boyer had nothing on Creepy Eddie. I broke it off with him and drove my Corolla back to where I came from.

When I was with them, I was convinced that each of these men was my prince. They all fulfilled Objective #1 of the above-outlined Quest. And maybe a couple even got around to Objective #2 and loved me in their way. As for #3? They never changed, never stayed. But I had changed . . . into a delusional, desperate, clingy stalker. It killed me to think it, but maybe my mother was right.

My Airport Epiphany

It's embarrassing to admit, but all the way up to and through my college years, I harbored the fantasy that my father would return to me. He would show up on my doorstep full of heartfelt apologies, a changed man, willing to take on the job of staying and loving me forever. Hence, The Quest, because if he didn't do it, *someone* should.

In the years after my parents' divorce, I rarely heard from or saw my father. One occasion was at my grandmother's funeral, when I was thirteen. I watched him cry over his mother and then, figuring he was really feeling the parent/child bond thing, begged him to take me with him. He said nothing, barely looked at me, and disappeared again. A cloak of rejection and a feeling of utter invisibility haunted me from that moment on. I didn't see him again during my childhood.

Then, when I was twenty-five, in a bold and unusual move, he called *me* and wanted to *see me*. But now I was a woman. I thought that I was mature and over his abandonment, so I agreed to his visit. I'm cool. It's cool. We're cool.

Driving to the airport to pick him up, I gave myself a pep talk. "You can do this, he's your father and he's reaching out." I stood at the gate as his flight arrived and passengers were filing off the plane. I realized that I didn't know what he looked like, so I tried to draw a mental picture of him.

I muttered to myself under my breath while I scanned the

crowd, "He's much older now, his hair is probably gray. He might be hunched over. Heck, I was six inches shorter the last time I saw him, so I might even be taller than him. If he's just a little old man, don't look shocked." These were my thoughts when Cupid's arrow shot me straight through the heart.

This gorgeous guy was getting off the plane. He had his sunglasses on indoors, a leather jacket, and a confident swagger. I completely forgot why I was there. *"Wow, who is that hot guy?"* I honed in on him, my body viscerally pulled in that love-at-first-sight, I'm-not-going-to-lose-him-in-this-crowd movie-moment kind of way, and as I got within twenty feet I realized *this guy* was my father.

Eeeeeww.

I shuddered. Oh no, I was not okay. In that moment, my unconscious Daddy Redemption Quest became a fully conscious slap in the face. I woke up to my neurosis and decided to abandon my Quest, **cold turkey.**

Chuck

My first attempt at a relationship with a non-daddy-like guy was with Chuck. Chuck was an angel, a sweet, cherubic beauty who was introduced to me by a mutual friend. He was loving, supportive, honest, and pure of heart. Worshiping me came easy to him and he showered me with kindness: leaving me a sweet note on my windshield, warming me with the sweater off his back, always making sure he walked on the street side of the sidewalk. Things I had never experienced before.

He was also a fantastic kisser, and I didn't let it go any further for a long time . . . because . . . well . . . uh . . . because . . . okay, because he had these teeny tiny hands and eentsy weentsy feet and I was terrified that he had a penis to match and that I would reject this sweetheart of a guy because of his penis size and that would make me a whole new kind of terrible person.

So I waited. For weeks I waited for him to do something cruel, but he just didn't seem to have it in him. Distasteful? Nothing, he was an absolute gentleman. Slightly insensitive? Never, he shooed spiders out of doors. I looked for *anything* that might justify me freaking out and leaving him in disgust. Nada, he was always honest, loving, and willing. We continued on for another blissful month while I tried to plot an unforgivable act so that *he* would leave *me*. All the while, we were getting to know each other, enjoying each other's company, and making out passionately on our dates. Once, we even found ourselves locked in a parking garage overnight because it closed around us during a marathon match of tonsil hockey.

But I would not go near his member. I kept my hands and my eyes away. I didn't want to know what was, or wasn't, there. We would break up eventually, right? And I was determined that it wasn't going to be because he was packing half a Hebrew National; it was going to be for a mature and legitimate reason.

Chuck mistook my waiting and chastity as, of all things, self-respect. And it only made him love me more and do more to earn the coveted prize of my precious flower. Yikes!

We were in dating purgatory for about two months when he gave me the best birthday of my life. He planned a camping excursion and he invited Angus, his friend's enormous German shepherd. All because I love dogs and I loved camping (sleeping on the ground has since lost its appeal) and I had told Chuck and he had actually paid attention.

He woke me up early on my birthday, told me to grab some warm clothes, my bikini, and my hiking boots, and we were off.

The mountain he chose was glorious! We swam in a crystal blue lake at the beginning of the hike. Chuck had packed all my favorite things and several small gifts and carried them on his back, pulling out one surprise after another along the way.

Hiking to our mountaintop campsite, we had to cross this rushing river over a log. But Angus, despite our urging—"Come on, Angus, you can do it, Angus! Angus, come!"—would NOT go over the log. So Chuck, and like I said, Chuck was sort of . . . dainty, he carried this behemoth animal through the cold rushing river, hip deep in the water, bracing himself against the log, using all the might he had in his teeny tiny hands.

Angus was not pleased, but Chuck had gotten him safely across to the other side, where Angus bounded off into the woods with no reward for Chuck. Now he was soaked, his shoes and socks squishing with every step as he beamed a smile at me and kissed me square on the mouth. "Nothing is going to spoil what I have planned for you, Cinderella."

This was an amazing guy. Not like my father at all and

real husband material. I didn't care if he had a pencil for a dick, I wanted him.

That night, in our little blue tent, we made love for the first time. And that's when I learned that even if the man wears elfin-sized gloves and shoes, you never know if you're going to get a pencil or a Pepsi can. Well, it wasn't exactly a Pepsi can, it was kind of like . . . a Red Bull maybe, with a little curve to the left . . . Anyway, I digress. It was fine, better than fine. I was worried for nothing.

On the hike back, when Angus got to the rushing river, he paused, looked back at us, and then trotted right over the log. Angus had learned that resistance only made things more difficult, and that it was pointless for them to both suffer because of his unreasonable fears. An epiphany that, as it turned out, gave that dog a big leg up on me.

On the drive home, I lay with my head in Chuck's lap and he gently stroked my face. When I looked up at him, his blond curls were ignited by the movement of the sun through the trees. It looked like an electric halo, a blaring siren of a sign, in case I still needed one. His lips turned up into a gentle smile and out of nowhere he said, "I love you, you know."

Whoa. What am I supposed to do with that? I took a deep inhale and closed my eyes. He made me peaceful inside and our relationship had a clean, pure feeling to it. I felt an urgent tug from the evolved part of my soul: *"Come on, Cindy, you can do it, Cindy! Cindy, COME!"* I pondered. Could I overcome my crippling fears of intimacy and cross the metaphorical log? I mean, maybe this was love. Of course, it didn't feel anything like what I understood love to be, what with all its painlessness and joy. It was utterly foreign in that it lacked both constant suspicion and that delicious desperation of not knowing how he felt about me. Hmmm. Yeah, okay, what the hell, I'll give it a try. How hard could it be? Sure, I could attempt to love a man that was *already a good person*.

"I love you, too," I finally replied, in acknowledgment of the possibility that love comes in many forms. Perhaps this feeling, this purity and peacefulness, despite my complete unfamiliarity with it, was one of them. I was, of all things, happy.

Unfortunately for me, I had a condition known as "Low Bliss Tolerance" and that happiness made me deeply uncomfortable. In fact, his adoration made me queasy and was difficult to digest. The nicer he was to me, the barfier I got.

A week later, to my relief, my ex Creepy Eddie called me. He was full of regret and absolutely contrite. "Baby, I've been a liar, a cheat, a no-good son of a bitch. But I love you and I want to change so we can be together forever." And it awakened the beast in me. CUE THE CHOIR!!! AHA! An absolute cad, a two-timing perv, wanted me back! The elusive Objective #3 was being handed to me on a silver platter. He wanted to change his ways and love me forever. The only thing that stood between me and my unfinished Daddy Redemption Quest was Chuck.

I raced to Chuck's house. This had to be handled immediately.

"Chuck, Eddie wants me back," I blurted out.

"So?" Chuck responded.

"So, he wants to *change*." In my mind, this fact meant that breaking up with Chuck was the only course of action.

And Chuck, with deep compassion, sat down and pulled me next to him, taking both my hands in his. He said, "Wow, baby, I can see you have some unresolved issues. How about this—you can see him and you can work this out and I'll be here for you anytime. I'll wait for you to sort out your feelings. Just please don't sleep with him."

Chuck accepted me. He saw me. But I couldn't resist. "Oh God, Chuck. You are so sweet. *You just don't get it at all.*" And with that, I dumped Chuck. What about that evolved part of my soul? Well, it wasn't exactly running the show.

Eddie flew to me even though he hated to fly. He cried at my therapist's office with me even though he had never wanted to go to therapy. We had ecstatic victory sex, and he did everything right and I was ready to throw myself a friggin' ticker-tape parade!

And then, after two weeks of perfectly fulfilling Objective #3, Eddie gave up, told me it was too hard, left me and returned home to Gilda and a life with no ankles. He would not change. He would not stay. I failed again.

But my depression was short-lived, because I remembered that dear, sweet Chuck loved me! I picked myself up and dusted myself off for what I thought would be a tender reunion.

I went to him looking cute and contrite and said, "Chuck, I've made a terrible mistake, but I'm back and I'm all yours . . ."

He lit up and spread his arms out wide, thrusting his pure heart forward. "Oh, babe! I'm so happy! I was really worried you were going to sleep with him."

THUD. I squirmed. It would be best now to just throw myself into his embrace, to let him shower me with kisses and regale him with a prizewinning sex-a-thon. But there was something about him, about that damn purity, that made it impossible to lie to him, even a lie of omission. But he would understand, right? I'm damaged, I'm working my shit out. He loves that about me.

"Um, I did sleep with him," I confessed quietly, and then quickly followed it with "But I get it now. You are a good man, a wonderful man, and Eddie is an icky bad man, and I want to be with *you*."

He wanted to take me in his arms, I could tell, but something in him just wouldn't let him do it. It was, of all things, self-respect. He just heaved a big sigh, and a single streaming tear rolled down his cherub cheek. "I love you, I really do. I . . . I just can't be with a woman who doesn't respect herself. We had something going that was so pure, and now that you've had sex with Eddie, it's ruined. I'm sorry, Princess." And with that, Chuck escorted me to the door.

Despite numerous and desperate attempts on my part to win him back, which included trying to kidnap Angus and holding his favorite sweater hostage, Chuck stayed away.

Chuck was taking care of himself. Of course, someone with self-respect knows how to do such things. He understood that if I didn't know how to honor myself, I would never be able to honor him or our relationship. And Chuck was right.

Anytime I attempt to break a bad habit, just when I start to feel cocky about it, the universe conspires to test me. It tempts me with the very thing I am trying to live without. Sadly, I snatched at Eddie and my freaky little Quest without even considering the consequential loss: the love of a truly good man.

But I just couldn't give it up. My Daddy Redemption Quest was like crack, and now I knew I had a serious problem. But if good Chuck didn't understand and if good Chuck wouldn't take me back, then I was going back on the pipe.

Romeo

Romeo smelled like bacon, booze, and coconut oil. His regular uniform was to go shirtless, wearing only camouflage shorts and clogs, if he wore any shoes at all. He got away with it because his toned, hairless, hazelnut-colored torso was carefully fashioned for public viewing.

The first thing I did when we met, before we had exchanged a single word, was slide a ripe summer strawberry in his mouth, and he accepted it until there was nothing between my fingers and his lips except those tiny little leaves. Oh, it was on. The first night we spent together was full of flowing bourbon, oozing plates of pork fat, and a dense pot haze. And then we had our first taste of our favorite indulgence, this-might-be-the-last-time-I-ever-see-you sex. He told me the next morning that he was "allergic to monogamy" *and* an alcoholic. PERFECT! Romeo became the ultimate Quest subject.

He tortured me with expert finesse, openly sleeping with

me, then my neighbor, then back to me, then our random cocktail waitress for the evening, then back to me, then (and this is my favorite) another girl named Cindy so that when he came back to me and called out my name during sex, I could still suspect he was thinking of someone else.

He was always disappearing, standing me up, forgetting that he said he loved me while he was getting blackout drunk. The back of his head was his best feature, and he showed it to me again and again. **He was the sexiest man alive.** Being with him was intoxicating, because in that moment he was choosing *me*, and *this* time he would stay and I was one step closer to slaying my dragon! I focused my Cad-Changer Laser Beam on him and tried to grip him with my Stay-With-Me-Forever Death Claws. But he was a good and worthy opponent. He would not give in, would not change, would not stay.

In one of our epic, deliciously painful shrieking (me)/ avoiding (him) fests, he finally laid it out for me.

"Listen, Lu"—which he was now calling me so as to distinguish me from the other Cindy—"I can't give you what you need! You're just too much for one man to handle."

"Oh really. How many men would it take?" I spat back sarcastically.

And after a long moment of actually thinking about it, looking up and away like he was truly calculating, he answered, **"Four."**

"Oh, okay." At the time, I didn't really get what he was saying. That my needs and my expectations were so high that no one man, certainly not a man so carefully selected for

his devastating flaws, could handle them. All I understood was that I had failed in my Quest AGAIN.

So in a fit of self-destructive determination to make him pay, I fucked him. Then his coworker. Then him again, then his basketball buddy, back to him, then our mutual friend and neighbor. And then I told him all about it over a glass of Chianti.

"There!" I sipped smugly. "That makes four."

"Geez, Lu, that really hurts," he confessed.

"Yeees! You see!? This is why we should be in a monoga-mous relationship!" I was elated! He understood my pain and how silly and unnecessary it was, and now we could move forward.

"But, Lu, I can't be monogamous with you now. You slept with all my friends."

Oh, for fuck's sake. My revenge sex plan had completely backfired.

So I moved on to the "I'm no better than you" approach. I tried to out-drink him, out-smoke him, out-sleaze him. If our relationship couldn't make him a better man, then I would adopt the worst parts of him. Maybe that would tie us together forever, I thought. I was so hell-bent on fulfilling my Daddy Redemption Quest that I would destroy us both.

One cannot take a coyote as a pet and then be angry at it when it kills one's cat. It is simply in its nature.

When I looked behind me at the destruction in my wake, I realized that the Quest was eating me alive. I was breaking myself into pieces and giving them away all over the place.

I was a crack whore for love. I needed help.

3. MATH AND SCIENCE TO THE RESCUE

How I went from Love Junkie to Lab Monkey

"Problems cannot be solved by using the same kind of thinking we used when we created them."

—ALBERT E.

I'm Chinese.
We're Good at Math.

I sucked at love. It was long past time to admit that. But I *love love*. It's my favorite. I could take a little break from it, but it wasn't something I could give up. I just wanted to love in a way that made sense, that didn't hurt so many people, particularly myself. I wanted to be smart about it.

Could I use anything I learned in school? There was a class called Sexual Education, but all I learned there was that putting condoms on bananas was a waste of condoms and bananas. Then I remembered that from algebra to calculus, from biology to anatomy, all of my teachers had gushed: "You're such a natural! You really should think about pursuing a career in math and science!" I'm Asian and I wore thick glasses and got straight A's, so for them it was like telling a seven-foot freshman he should think about going for a basketball scholarship. But what the heck, I was definitely better at math and science than I was at love.

I decided to fire the emotionally imbalanced, damaged, and destructive daddy-questing junkie and put my Math and Science Team in charge of my love life and my vagina.

In math and science, systems are built off of theories. The proof of a theory's validity lies in the collection of data and the charting of results. The obsessions, quests, and psychological makeup of the experimenter are, at best, side notes. I admit, they may be the driving force behind the nature of the experiment, but they do not change the results. Luckily for you.

Through a series of test men and experimental dates, analyzing previously accumulated data and using myself and girlfriends as guinea pigs, I developed a systematic formula for love that can be used by dysfunctional Cinderellas of all ages. My Theory of Lovitivity.

I call that system THE FOUR MAN PLAN.

 Doesn't applying math and science to love take all the romance out of it?

Consider this:

- The rhythm and melodies of music are accomplished through an understanding of math.
- Art appreciation can be explained through the scientific principles of space relation and color combination.
- Design mirrors nature with its symmetry and geometric shapes.
- Infinite space is quantified through physics.

Why should love be any different?

By looking at love through the lens of math and science, I discovered that a system already existed. Romance is not random, love is not chaos. There are proven methods that yield reliable results. The professors in this field are our mothers and grandmothers, our married, divorced, and widowed coworkers, friends, and confidants. Their knowledge of this system is more commonly known as *hindsight*. And by learning from them and our own personal experiences, we can increase our understanding of love and attract more of it into our lives.

The Four Man Plan diagrams their wisdom into an easy-to-use graphable format with concrete calculations. This way, we can put our capable minds in the driver's seat instead of continuing to let our wounded hearts and indiscriminate vaginas careen us through the backwoods of love.

Now let's get to work.

4. THE THEORIES BEHIND THE 4MP

Myth vs. Math

"It is the theory that decides what we can observe."

—AL

The Theories Behind The 4MP

As I stated earlier, in math and science, systems are built off of theories. First a theory is created and then it is tested and observed for accuracy. I thought it wise to sort through my old unsuccessful theories about the search for love. Even though the outmoded theories I had accumulated were popular notions, by my observation they DID NOT lead to the desired result, $u+1$ (or, since it was me experimenting on me, $i+1$), and therefore were fully proven as *inaccurate* and should be tossed out the stinking window. I then decided to pinpoint the opposite argument and throw that up against the wall to see if my spaghetti was getting cooked.

The following collection of metaphors and theories are the building blocks of The Four Man Plan. My earlier beliefs about love were the antithesis of these six proven methods for capturing the elusive. These new concepts gave me the blueprint to observe and correct my many repeated errors committed in my pursuit of balanced and lasting love. If you find yourself squirming your way through The Plan, review these theories to get your legs back.

4MP and Pets

Do you have dogs? Do you watch Cesar Milan's *The Dog Whisperer* on the National Geographic Channel? I love that guy. And if you watch the program closely, you realize that he's not just talking about how to train dogs. He's talking about how to win at life. "Calm and Assertive," that's his mantra. "Always be Calm and Assertive."

He denounces our desire to treat our dogs like human children, friends, and spouses. He stresses that the one thing that makes your dog the happiest is that you treat it *like a dog.* They have their own psychology based on their instincts as pack animals and predators. They have their own rules to live by and their own emotional triggers that are different from a human's. But since we have invited dogs to live in our human world, the best courtesy we can pay them is to understand them for who they are and ask them to join us without requiring them to become one of us. Instead, to live in harmony we have to integrate their rules of life with our own.*

Dogs respond instantly to their own language no matter who is speaking it. They are more responsive to a stranger who speaks to them in Dogtalk than a loved one speaking Human.

What does this have to do with dating? Now, I'm not saying men are dogs. I'm just saying, are we sure we should be treating them as the same species as us? And wouldn't it be easier to learn the rather simple and predictable language of

---

*There's one more point to make about Love and Animals. As much as we can love our pets to pieces and they never tire of our company, they cannot replace a human relationship. Denying this can be a dangerous, long, dark road that leads to endless games of fetch and months without sex or meaningful human contact. Admit it, the conversations are a bit one-sided, and your pet may never forgive you for having him neutered. Repeat after me: **My dog is not my boyfriend.** (Neither is your cat, your bird, your iguana, etc.)

Manspeak than to seek out a Man who understands the overly nuanced and complex Womanese?

The 4MP is structured around male psychology and instincts. So for a man looking for love, finding a 4MPlanner is like finding a fellow American when he has been forced to live in France.

ERROR

I need to find a man who understands me.

Correction: It is far more within my control to learn to understand another and communicate in his language.

4MP and Casino Management

Some of the best-run and consistently successful businesses in the world are casinos. They are built on the backs of losers and everyone knows it; and yet people the world over continue to gamble and casinos continue to take their money. How can that be? Because it is an industry built on the art of blending *reliable human behavior* with the *certainty of math*.

The reliable behavior is this: *Humans are an optimistic species.* And we consider a chance to be optimistic as entertainment. So even if we know that Vegas is designed for us to lose our money gambling, we go with the understanding that *some* people win and we enjoy considering ourselves in that category.

The mathematical certainty is this: *The odds are in the casino's favor.* Casinos know that for every bet played, they win sixteen and lose fifteen, give or take, depending on the game. The more bets made, the more dollars gambled, the more the casino is guaranteed its percentage. There is no luck involved, and the house always wins. Not from every single player, but every single day given that they lure enough people in to play. Thus, the groovy lights, the bargain meals, and the spectacular shows.

With The Four Man Plan, you become the casino of dating and wield the power that blends *reliable human behavior* with *the certainty of math.* To be a guaranteed winner, find a way to be the house that is appealing enough to attract the requisite number of players to guarantee your winnings. Players need luck to win, the casino does not, and that is how you can use math to redesign your fantasies and turn them into realities.

ERROR

I only have one soul mate.

Correction: There are 6.6 billion people in the world. The number of people who have claimed to have found their soul mate suggests that there are lots and lots of people who can delight my soul. So to put the odds in my favor, I must get out there and meet as many of them as possible.

4MP and Killer Abs

After years of mostly yoga, hiking, and a few gym visits here and there as exercise, I thought it was just my lot in life to have a flat ass and soupy, flappy underarms, but basically I felt pretty good. Once I hit my thirties, though, I peppered in a bit of stress and an attachment to cheese plates and my health started to take a slide. Then one day I noticed a sign up at my gym advertising personal trainers that said, "If you can't make time for health, make time for illness." I thought I knew the basic principles behind staying in shape, but I figured I'd see what a little instruction could do for me.

Bridgette, my personal trainer, was hard-core. During workouts I often suspected she was trying to kill me and would frequently ask her, "Who sent you?" between reps. She extolled the virtues of pain: that pushing our muscles past the point of pain and exhaustion is the only way to make them stronger. Break them down to build them up. It was after many months of working out and following what seemed like an unreasonable regimen that I felt this muscle in my shoulder that I never had before. I showed it to her. "Oh, that's your medial deltoid," she told me. I didn't even know what a medial deltoid was, much less that I had two of them waiting to be developed. They were an additional bonus to having a surprisingly pert ass, killer abs, and slightly less flappy (but still flappy, DAMN YOU, YIN FAMILY CURSE!) upper arms.

One day, I knew something about me had changed when I was riding a bike on the beach. I looked up at a staircase that was so steep and long I could not see the top of it. My body responded *with delight* at the sight. I hopped off my bike and ran up it, taking two and three stairs at a time, and then when I reached the top I jumped up and down and belted out a self-congratulatory "Whoohoo!" Oh man, it felt so great. I did it again. Bizarre, right?

Even though I am ultimately a yoga girl, I do not regret the time I spent in the gym with Bridgette and learned what my body had to offer if I choose to work my ass off.

The Four Man Plan is a love fitness program. Like a physical fitness program, you have to be committed to it for a period of time to truly experience the benefits. Even if it makes you uncomfortable, even if it hurts. It will take time to see results, and day by day you may not notice them. But as long as you keep working at it, they are happening. I've never made any forward progress anywhere in my life without trying something that threw me outside of my comfort zone. And it has always been worth it. Aren't love and health running neck and neck as the two best things to have and, therefore, the most important things to work on? You may discover something that was always within you just waiting to be developed. And once you know what is possible, you cannot un-know it.

ERROR

I'm just not good at dating.

Correction: The thing I desire most may reside at the end of a lot of hard work in an area in which I am initially incompetent or would rather not do. Get comfortable with being uncomfortable and my dreams will be at my fingertips.

4MP and Sports

The sport The Four Man Plan most resembles is golf. Each player, or in the case of The 4MP each Plan Man, is on the course simultaneously, doing his individual best. Every once in a while, a glance at the leader board or a roar from a distant crowd lets them know that they better step up their game. This is a gentleman's game of finesse and self-regulation, not a contact sport.

As soon as they are old enough to toddle, most boys are taught two things: good sportsmanship and how to play with balls. They learn to follow sets of rules that change from game to game. They experience winning or losing through a difference that can be measured in inches, seconds, and points. Some boys are taught to do their best and some are trained to win. Either way, the joy of competing in a game with structure and boundaries is ingrained in their minds and hearts.

But most boys aren't really taught how to make a girl feel special. Fathers don't usually spend quality time teaching their sons that love is active, not just a feeling. Every boy hears the line "It's not whether you win or lose, it's how you play the game." But there's not a lot of "Come on, son, let's do laundry together to show Mom how much we appreciate her."

You cannot force men to understand the complicated and ever-changing world of female emotions and needs. So why not learn their far simpler world of sports and game strategy, with its concrete scoring and judgments and easily discernible winners and losers? Once you've structured love into a format they can understand, let them do what they do best: learn complex strategies, figure out their strengths and weaknesses, and design playbooks that edge out the competition.

As a 4MPlanner you will not be playing within the game of love. You are not competing against the men you seek *or* other women. Instead, you will be taking on the roles of the cheerleader, the coach, the referee, and the president of the league. Let them play their hearts out to win the big prize: YOU!

This line of thinking is the root of why The Plan Man, at a certain point, must know that he is competing with other men for your affections. Now it's not just dating, it's a sport!

ERROR

A man will lose interest if I make him compete for me.

Correction: Men thrive on competition. All competition is merely a structure within which one's achievements and abilities can be measured. And there is nothing men love more than being measured.

4MP and My Cute Jeans

I have at least twelve pairs of jeans. You know, the one that goes with boots, the one that works with halter tops, dark rinsed, light washed, fancy pockets, plain pockets, in all sizes for every time of the month. But there is only one pair that I wear every week, only casting them aside when they are destined for laundry, and even then they've been dug out and worn for emergencies. They are my comfortable *and* cute, dress up, dress down, make-my-ass-look-great jeans. Do you have that one special pair? Did you know they were The Ones when you bought them? I didn't. Mine are Lucky Brands, a brand I had never worn before that I got at Loehmann's just to get a pair cheap so I could get out of a gorgeous but ridiculously uncomfortable pencil skirt I was wearing. These jeans weren't even the stretchy kind, which is a quality that I had grown very attached to in any form of denim.

Who knows how they ended up at Loehmann's, but it's got to be because someone returned them, they were deemed out of fashion, or something was wrong with them. Even with all those strikes against them, they are my favorite. Over all my other carefully selected jeans, some very expensive and from fancy stores, I would wear my Lucky Brands every day if I could. I want to be an old lady wearing them, even when they are horribly out of style. I want to marry them.

The point being, everyone needs jeans. A few of us are lucky enough to find the perfect pair. I found mine in the reject section of the out-of-season store.

The Plan is designed to prove that the most unassuming guy, found in the unlikeliest of places, lacking your most important requirements, could be the one you always wanted and didn't know it. The important thing is to keep looking, because they are not going to jump onto your ass on their own.

ERROR

I know my type.

Correction: Sometimes what you are looking for is unlike anything you have ever seen and is tucked away in a place you may have never guessed to search.

4MP and Money

When it comes to investing for the long term, individual stocks are for the birds. Let's say you put all your money into one stock—for example, NETFLIX. If you watch that stock's activity several times every day, focusing all your attention on it, hoping to make it responsible for your future security, trust me, you will be miserable. A single stock jumps and dives and will make your stomach turn. But it's just doing what stocks do. An overly focused interest in it is not going to change its progress; it's only going to waste your time and give you mini anxiety attacks.

There will be days when you have no faith in it at all and want to bail out. There will be days of false hope when you think it's going to provide you with everything you need. That's a lot of pressure for a little company that's just trying to make it in the world. If you called the people at NETFLIX and told them that you had all your money in them and you were counting on them succeeding to make your life better, even they would tell you . . . **"Diversify your portfolio."**

The Four Man Plan allows you to diversify your love portfolio and raises your "risk tolerance" with each Plan Man.

Don't lower your expectations, but divide them and increase your overall potential for reaching your goals. Every man you add to The Plan helps you distribute the pressure for each individual man to perform to your satisfaction. If you have four potential dates on Valentine's Day, or six possible rides to the airport, your needs will most likely get met. The fun part is in the surprise of who meets them.

In the future, one Plan Man may end up being a tenbagger who pays off long into retirement, but for now, enjoy the peace of mind that comes from a balanced portfolio.

ERROR

I like to focus on one man at a time.

Correction: A watched pot never boils. Okay, it does, but it hates being watched.

5. THE POSTULATES OF THE 4MP

Postulate: *n.* 1. something that is assumed or believed to be true and that is used as the basis of an argument or theory 2. an essential precondition or requirement

The acceptance of these postulates is required for success with The 4MP.

"Things should be made as simple as possible, but not any simpler."

—EINSTEIN

The Postulates of The 4MP

Here's what I love about postulates: By definition they do not have to be self-evident or even provable. In math and science, a chain of logic has to begin from somewhere to keep it from being infinite and circular (like some of our dating dramas). Therefore, any mathematical or logical system is defined by a set of postulates. Are you starting to get the feeling that I'm dead serious about this whole using-math-to-find-love thing? Good, because I totally am!

The following five postulates are the starting point for the system that is The 4MP, and in order for it to work they must be embraced as true by each individual 4MPlanner. You might not fully agree with them or have any personal connection to them. You might even get mad at them. But that doesn't really matter. Just like in ninth-grade geometry class, your duty as a 4MPlanner is to commit these postulates to memory and repeat them to yourself when doing The Plan gets difficult and makes you want to stick a protractor in your eye.

The Distribution of Love

Postulate #1: Assume that you are in the majority.

Some people win the Lotto, some people are discovered in a soda shop, and some people experience love at first sight that results in lifelong blissful marriages. If you are reading this book, that is probably not you.

Polls indicate (that would mean me asking about twenty of my friends) that love at first sight happens to about 50 percent of all people.

Of that 50 percent, the feeling is mutual and results in a happy relationship . . . oh, let's be generous and say 10 percent of the time. Ten percent of 50 percent equals 5 percent total (or one very lucky girlfriend).

Another 5 percent of all people are truly meant to be alone. You know who they are and, hopefully, they know who they are (one cranky meth-head neighbor).

Therefore, for 90 percent of the population, your best chance at love is something OTHER than love at first sight. I know that's very sad to hear, and I'm not saying you're not that one-in-twenty girl. But just in case you're not, there's plenty of other ways to find your guy. So instead of sitting around waiting for love at first sight to club you over the head, let yourself get a little perked up when you meet someone you don't like right away. Now, that guy has mathematical potential!

Distribution of Love Pie Chart

Postulate #1

Lone Wolves

Happy Relationships
As a result of
Love at First Sight

No Love at
First Sight

Experience
Love at First Sight

The Rest of Us

The Disney Theorem

Postulate #2: When it comes to competing for love there is a big difference between boys and girls.

A. When men compete for a woman it brings out the best in them: their innate chivalry, their good sportsmanship, their hibernating romantic. And as an added bonus, they grow into gentlemen whether they win the woman or not.

Example: *Snow White and the Seven Dwarfs*
Those little guys all loved her, doted on her, and remained friends even after she went off with that tall dude.

Example: *The Bachelorette*
The guys are suddenly writing love poems, and if they come in second, they become the best man at the wedding.

B. When women compete for a man, let's face it, ladies, it brings out the worst in us: We attack each other, we deny our true selves and generally feel like crap about it. Next thing you know, people are getting bitch slapped and private e-mails are being read, and we turn into suspicious, shrill, scared harpies. Whether we win the guy or not.

Example: **Cinderella**
Those stepsisters were just plain mean, locking poor Cinderella in the basement and trying to shove their boats in her tiny shoes. And as a result, they are not likely to be invited to the castle on holidays.

Example: **The Bachelor**
Competing girls sneak into the Bachelor's bedroom half naked to hock their wares and bad-mouth other girls.

Note that all of these examples are produced by Disney. Coincidence? Or should we blame it all on the cultural influence of cartoons and reality television? Alas, there is no corporate bully to point the finger at for this one.

It is a fact of nature that the most beautiful gender within any given species is the one to be fought over. In the case of peacocks, it is the males. In the case of humans, the beautiful ones are hands down the females. We all learn that for certain on our first misguided trip to a nude beach. Breasts are glowing orbs of lusciousness and ball sacs look like, well, warm gummy ball sacs. Needless to say, we're the pretty ones! Therefore, it is a natural instinctual response for men to compete for women but not the other way around.

But lately, by competing woman vs. woman for the same man, we keep lowering the bar for men. We plan the dates, we pick them up from their mom's house, we shorten our skirts and shrink-wrap our tits so they don't have to bother imaging what our naked bodies look like. We pay for the date and then we put out just so we can prove that we're a better bargain than that other girl. Men have to do less and less as women try to underbid one another. It's like we're all turning into that crazy mattress commercial guy: "I'll beat anyone's prices or your next blow job is FREEEEEEEEE!"

Let's stop the madness. It is completely unnatural and women, as a gender, are suffering. So, I don't mean to go all Norma Rae on your ass but LET'S UNIONIZE!

Therefore, The 4MP is *unidirectional*. It only works when the 4MPlanner is a woman or a gay man. Any way you cut it, the pursuers must be men. (You don't have to be Chinese, that's just a little picture of me.) You cannot be a 4MPlanner if you are a straight man or a lesbian. That would require an entirely different system.

The Disney Theorem

Postulate #2

Plan Men

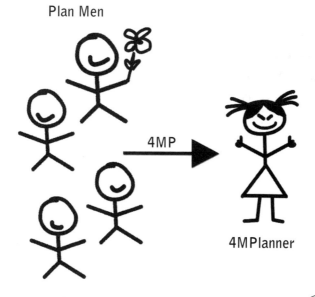

4MP

4MPlanner

The Wait for Sex Index

> **Postulate #3.** For the life of the relationship, men are only as nice to you as they need to be to get you in bed the first time.

Let's not forget our theory about The 4MP and Sports. Consciously or unconsciously, sex is the goal line for men. If you don't know how to put up some professional resistance, then you're really no fun to play with. A man will sleep with just about anybody, but he will fall in love with the woman who makes him feel like he's playing in the NFL.

Think of a man like a lion. Sex is part of his innate drive, and it is his biological imperative to pursue sex in order to keep the species alive. It is the human version of the hunt. It's what men's instincts tell them to do to stay alive. Sure, they seem to enjoy it if you're easy, they take what's given with an enthusiasm that we often mistake for true feelings. But by doing that you are turning what is supposed to be the king of the jungle into a zoo animal. The zoo lion saunters over to his food bin and just consumes what's handed to him, but his life is also unnatural and ultimately, innately unfulfilling. He may be fat and sated, but the zoo lion will always miss the hunt.

In the dating safari, if you are an easy kill, you're not even as rewarding as a wounded gazelle or a retarded bison—you're just a box of meat. Not a pretty picture, but what I'm really trying to say is: **Keep your damn knees together, sister!**

Know this: A man will almost always take whatever a woman offers. He is physically wired to do so, because he biologically cannot use his brain and have a boner at the same time. So when a woman is too easy, or even just falls for his persistent advances, here's what happens: He takes whatever sex he is given, leaves, and then when his weenie goes down, puts you into a category based on what you gave him. That's right, *he judges you.* **Even if he initiated the whole damn thing! EVEN IF HE BEGGED! YEP.** Now in his mind, he thinks you were an easy lay, you become one of *those girls*, and he'll always see you that way. Totally messed up, right?

What if he insists? Boohoo, that is just too bad for him. No matter what he expects, no matter how much he feels you led him on, it doesn't matter. Even if you asked him upstairs, took out his wee-wee for a look and sang into it like a microphone. I don't recommend letting it get that far, but even if it does, it's still your choice to stop the launch sequence. For the love of God, please don't have sex with a man out of obligation. It isn't something you trade for a shrimp cocktail and a show ticket. That's just creepy.

The Wait for Sex Index Graph

Postulate #3

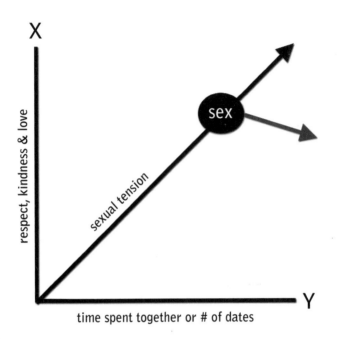

The **X axis** represents the level of **respect** and **caring** you receive from a man. This would include the opening of doors, the squashing of bugs, the listening to you. The **Y axis** represents the amount of **time spent together or # of dates** you go on. The "climax" occurs at the moment at which you have sex and is the point of diminishing returns.

The more time you spend with a man without having sex, the more you will intrigue him, the greater potential he will see in you, and the more he will do to get himself into the end zone. If he loses interest BEFORE you've had sex with him, you'll still be better off than if he dumps you AFTER you've had sex with him. Because if that is the case, then he was only interested in sex, and by not sleeping with him, you have successfully weeded him out without getting your hopes up and your feelings trampled.

What EXACTLY are you waiting for? This is not about being a cock tease or playing games. This is about self-preservation and forward motion in your love life. You are looking for something specific.

You are looking for a pattern of behavior that indicates a level of kindness and lovingness and integrity expressed by a man that satisfies what you would require in a husband or partner or boyfriend, whatever role you are looking to fill. There will be a bell that goes off in your head that says, "This is the kind of man I want to marry!" These actions do not necessarily need to be directed at you. They can be things that you discover about his character as you get to know each other. Chuck rang my bell when he carried that beast of a dog across that river. All of his other shortcomings (so to speak) became secondary to the fact that he was an amazing guy any woman would be lucky to have. And when you feel that way about a guy and have a sexual attraction to him, **release the hounds!**

What if you are horny as hell?

What if you just want to have sex with that cowboy at the bar who's in town for the rodeo, is that so wrong? Hey, I'm not your grandma! I want you to be able to shake your thing! So of course there is room in The Plan for that—keep reading, we'll get to it.

The Rule of Chuck

Postulate #4: A good guy will break up with you if he finds out you are whoring around.

When doing The 4MP, you must consider the possibility that each man entering The Plan may be "The One." (Or, as you will learn later, your 3½ Man.)

That being said, the future of each potential relationship must be protected. I ruined whatever potential happiness I had with Chuck (remember sweet, angel-faced Chuck from page 24?) not by considering Eddie, not even by seeing him and going to therapy with him. My future with Chuck was dashed the moment I had sex with Eddie. The purity of our relationship was lost.

And when it comes to the real thing, guys are very into purity, whether they admit it or not. If they are going to take the relationship seriously, they don't need to be the *first* guy you've ever been with, but they definitely want to be the

> **How much good would a Chuck fuck do if a good Chuck had small wood? He would fuck like a good Chuck could if a bad girl had done good.**

last guy you've slept with. With no one else in between. Otherwise, you've got Penis Cooties, which to them is incurable and makes you booty-call material but not wifey material.

Chuck respected himself enough to recognize that I was a liability and infected with Eddie Cooties. He dropped me like a hot potato.

This postulate helps us keep the good ones from exiting The Plan on their own because they think you are Slutty McSlutterson.

You Suck at Love

Postulate #5: Everything else you have tried to find health and balance in the area of love has not worked.

This postulate is something that you must own.

It doesn't mean that you have always sucked or do not have love in other areas of your life or that you are not a loving person in general. It just means that something in you is malfunctioning either when you are choosing men or trying to get closer to men or just trying to get out there at all.

To do The Plan, it doesn't really matter why you suck. But in my observation, it's either:

A. Your parents.

Whether they were neglectful or smothering, whether you witnessed their marriage or their divorce, whether they meant to screw you up or not, most of your love suckage can probably be traced back to good ol' Mom and Dad. Children can be a hard lot to please and have the ability to read the worst into a situation, blame themselves, and then turn it into an emotional steamer trunk that they will haul around for decades. Heck, it's hard NOT to get screwed up as a kid. Remember my devastating moment with my father at my grandmother's funeral? When I stood behind him and asked him to take me with him and he ignored me and walked away? I just recently found out, through some frank discussions with my father, that he lost much of his hearing when he was nineteen years old. So he didn't ignore my plaintive request made over my grandmother's grave—he couldn't HEAR ME. Even so, that was a seminal moment for me. It planted a seed of neurosis so deep that I blossomed into a boundaryless attention whore. Oops.

B. Arnie the Arsonist.

Arnie is that one guy who really did you in. He took all your budding self-esteem and blooming goddessness and pulled them right out of the ground. Even if you had the most perfect parents in the world, they could not protect you from the man who made you fall hard and then burned you and burned you good. After that, you either vowed that you'd never trust your heart to another man OR blamed yourself for not being good enough to keep him. Guess who loses?

So, no matter what you think your parents did or didn't do, or what that one guy did to you, at some point, the easiest way to get over it is to become completely responsible for your own love life. Do not repeat your mistakes, but also do not let them hold you back.

I do NOT suck at love!

If you are having trouble with this one, contact your five closest confidants and ask them this simple yes/no question: "Do I suck at love?" Record their answer and take the majority ruling. If one of them gave you this book, count it as two points. I'll wait here. . . .

Okay, are the votes in? Do you suck? Great!

So hear this: Your reasons for sucking are not as important as moving forward. When you know you suck at something you really want to excel at, your best course of action is to humble yourself, question your old methods, and ask for help. Maybe even follow a system that has proven successful for other fellow love suckers.

So why not give The Four Man Plan a whack? After all, there is only so much growth you can do on your own or in a therapist's office without the benefit and the risk of interacting with actual men.

Each Plan Man will give you an opportunity for self-awareness. Something about them or what they do will push your buttons, and that is where you get your opportunities to grow. And generally speaking, any man who helps you understand yourself will win a place in your heart.

YOU SUCK AT LOVE

6. DATA COLLECTION

Don your lab coats, ladies, it's time to get down and dirty.

"Our task must be to free ourselves by widening our circle of compassion to embrace all living creatures and the whole of nature and its beauty."

—A.E.

Data Collection

Everyone knows that we as humans use less than 10 percent of our brains, but it is also likely that we are using less than an effective amount of our hearts, and that may be what's keeping your love life in a holding pattern. The following exercises will prepare you for your time on The Plan. They are designed to stretch your heart muscles, sculpt your mindset, and whip your vagina into shape.

Exercise 1:
Deal-Breaker Inclusion

Write a list of your deal-breaking or turn-off qualities in a man. *Examples:* men under six feet tall, mimes, vegans, etc.

1.

2.

3.

4.

5.

6.

7.

8.

9.

10.

Dig deep. I know there's more stuff that bugs the crap out of you!

11.

12.

13.

14.

Now that you are clear about what qualities you have deemed unacceptable in the past, embrace the fact that the man you will love with all your heart will have *at least one or more* of these qualities. In fact, nature has a real sense of humor about this one.

While on The Plan, you are not allowed to reject men for any of your deal-breaker qualities unless they are also outlined in The Breakup Ladder on page 131. So eat some tofu for strength and dust off your flats—the man of your dreams may be stuck in an invisible box.

Exercise 2:
Expectation List

Next, write a list of your must-have and desirable qualities in a man, and don't be afraid to get a little shallow and specific. *Examples:* handsome, successful, sexy, charming, can fix things, drives a nice car, makes a great margarita, etc.

1.

2.

3.

4.

5.

6.

7.

8.

9.

10.

11.

12.

13. HONEST

14. LOVING

15. WILLING

Expectation Reduction

Okay, so even though you have just listed a dozen or more of your expectations and that list is often followed by the plea *"Is that so much to ask for?,"* while you are on The Plan you will be focusing on the last three. Highlight them, circle them, memorize them. **Honest, loving, and willing are the three qualities that trump all others when you are seeking out your Plan Men.** Learn how to determine if a Plan Man has these qualities quickly and you will be that much further ahead of the game.

For those of you who are unfamiliar with these qualities, here is what they look like:

HONEST = RELIABLE DATA

He is where he says he is.
He is who he says he is.
He shares his truth.

More than anything, reliable data keeps us sane and on track. Someone who is truthful with you will not always please you, but they respect you and your connection. Honesty brings dignity to your relationship, even if times are tough or things don't work out. If you're the naturally suspicious type, as I was, always start out by trusting a Plan Man's honesty. If he's not the honest type, your trust will really screw with his head and he will eventually trip up or clean up his act on his own. Trust inspires trustworthiness.

LOVING = POSITIVE EXPERIENCES

He holds your hand.
He listens to you.
He supports you in your specialness.

When you're on the lookout for loving, it's the little things that matter. Sweeping gestures of romance are nice, but it's the guy who will walk your dog when you're stuck at work or suggests you order *both* desserts or lets you vent about your lousy day who's the real keeper.

WILLING = POTENTIAL ENERGY

He is willing to try yoga with you.
He is willing to not sleep with you right away.
He is willing to examine himself and his environment.

Willingness can cancel out almost any flaw or dealbreaker. People who are willing are curious about the world and interested in their own growth. And when that curiosity includes attention and interest in a love relationship, that's some of the best fun you can have. Willing means he's your classic "Come With Guy." As long as your requests are reasonable, he comes with you to look at paint swatches, he comes with you to your nephew's birthday party, he comes with you to face that mean mechanic, all because he wants to. Glorious.

Your best chance at attracting men with these qualities is

to be conscious about having them yourself. For a successful, fulfilling long-term relationship, these three qualities are essential. Whether or not he's got a trust fund or looks good in leather pants is going to have to go on the back burner and be considered extra credit.

Exercise 3:
A Powwow with Your Hoo-ha

Wrap your brain around this one:

You and your vagina are two separate entities with separate opinions about whom you want to have sex with and who you want to have relationships with.

Huh?

Have you ever found yourself having a torturous relationship with a man who was making you insane but you stuck around because the sex was SO HOT? *Answer: Who is Romeo?* Guess who was keeping me in that nightmare? My vagina. She LOVED him. She wanted to MARRY him. And for years I let her run roughshod over my love life.

If the main reason that you suck at love is that you just can't pick 'em, you might want to think about who's been calling the shots. It's time to have a powwow with your hoo-ha. Gently break it to her that you will be heading the committee from now on and negotiate a peaceful understanding. Like any good companion, her opinions matter, but let's not forget that she can be an indiscriminate pleasure seeker and a real bitch with a grudge. You should value her responses and give them careful consideration. In the end, she should get approval on your final choice. But ultimately, she should not be the Chairman of the Bed.

Sit Down, Va-Jay-Jay!

Now, I'm not saying not to give her love. Put her on the pedestal she deserves. Protect her and treat her as the precious, delicate rosebud that she is, and when the timing is right and you are both in agreement . . . oh, oh, oooooooooOOOH! What great fun the two of you can have together.

7. THE MANTRIS GRAPH

Your twenty-first-century dance card.

"Not everything that counts can be counted, and not everything that is counted counts."

—AL

The Mantris Graph

> *A 4MPlanner's mission is to fill her Mantris Graph with various values of Plan Men* **without going over.**

The Mantris Graph and the variable values of Plan Men are the centerpiece, the beating heart of The 4MP. The Mantris Graph allows you to keep track of your Plan Men and chart your progress. Consider it your blank canvas. Guaranteed, your Graph will be an original and, in time, high art.

8. THE PLAN MEN

All Plan Men are not created equal. Each Plan
Man qualifies for one of four basic values,
with a maximum total of four Whole Men.

Here come the boys!

"Let every man be respected
as an individual and no man
idolized."

—MR. E.

The Quarter Man

Any man who shows an interest in you, or you might like to go out with, any man you manage to exchange a phone number or an e-mail address with, starts off as a **Quarter Man.**

REQUIREMENTS: You know his name, his single status, and a way to contact each other.

These are the guys you know have a crush on you, but you think "No way" or "Yeah, but . . ."

These are the guys you have been eyeing but don't think you have a chance in hell with.

These are the guys who are not your type, you don't think you have the time for, are too short, too broke, too sweet, too hairy, too quiet, too toothy, WHATEVER. If you have room for them, then they go in the graph.

You do not need to like them.

You do not need to see potential.

You don't even really get to pick unless your Mantris Graph is full.

Why would I want to interact with men I don't necessarily like?

Because, dear 4MPlanner, let's say it's poker you suck at instead of love. If you want to learn to play poker, you'll be a lot happier if you learn to play with quarters and not $100 chips. You can afford to lose a few quarters by screwing up, taking risks, and trying out new techniques on your path to being a card shark. Playing with quarters makes the game relatively painless and still fun.

So go about casually collecting Quarter Men like you collect quarters. When you see one that is unclaimed, pick it up. Accept them when they are handed to you. When you lose one in the soda machine, kick it to see if it will spit a different one out. Keep a few in your pocket. They are no big deal. They may not seem to have much value, but you never know when a Quarter will finish your laundry, give you thirty extra meter minutes, or scratch off the silver stuff on a winning lottery ticket. On any given day, Quarters can save your friggin' life in some small way. Love your Quarters.

A stranger / casual acquaintance / friend of a friend / online prospect, etc., becomes a Quarter Man the moment you exchange a way to contact each other. **You are allowed to make first contact. In fact, if there is someone you've been eyeing up for months and haven't had the girl stuff to approach, consider him your first homework assignment.**

The Plan is not about being aloof. If you dig him and you want to call, call. ONCE. If you do not dig him, give him your number anyway and wait for him to call you.

A man loses his Quarter Man status if he does not contact you for two weeks. He may be reassigned as a Quarter if he contacts you later—if you have room for him in your Mantris Graph.

He remains a Quarter Man until he is promoted when after at least one date you tell him that you are seeing other men (Half Man) or until you let him feel your boobies (Whole Man) or hide his salami (Two and a Quarter Man).

Quarter Man Visuals

 = the 1/4 Man

OR

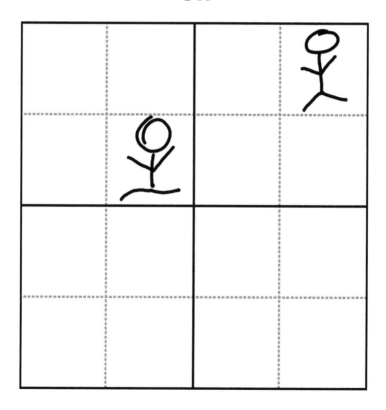

Methods of Collection

There are all sorts of shenanigans that women go through to meet a man. There are "techniques" to get someone to know you're interested. They include lingering eye contact, pretending to share interests, and invading personal space to get them to initiate conversation. Although I think that does work sometimes, there is a high failure rate, and if you ask me, it's game playing. Also, beware a man who is too tuned in to "signals"; he is more likely to be the predator or player type.

For the most part, HONEST, LOVING, and WILLING men are out minding their own business and not constantly trolling for women. This is the breed of men we are trying to give confidence to and coax out of hiding. That will require a direct approach.

When it comes to meeting new men, get courageous and casual at the same time. Turn on your "HOT DOUGH-NUTS" sign and open up the doors. Success comes to those who create opportunities for themselves. Sign up for classes you're interested in, like French Cooking or Argentinian Tango. Show up for church, have lunch with people from work, reply yes to evites, and do charity work. Deepen your involvement in your hobbies and interests. Tell your friends and family you are willing to be set up and you will be surprised how many available men there are. Keep your eyes peeled! A woman on the hunt for a husband can be repellent, but a girl looking for a date smells like freshly baked pastries.

How to Collect Quarter Men

1. Before leaving the house, make sure you have business cards or premade slips of paper with your e-mail address on them. A prepared 4MPlanner is a busy 4MPlanner!

2. You spot a potential Plan Man, walk right up to him, and:
    a. comment on your environment
    b. give him a compliment
    c. ask his opinion about something
    d. ask him a question
    e. all of the above

    Be creative, be charming, be brave. It will only be hard the first few times you try it.

3. Next, stick your hand out and say, "Hi, my name is (*your name here*)." Add a firm, inviting handshake and a "What's your name?"
    This can be done when you are behind him in the coffee line, next to him on the bus, or on a crowded dance floor under the half-naked go-go dancer.

4. Then, even if you don't have a conversation, or the one you have is awkward and uncomfortable, or he blows your mind and you think you're in love, reach into your pocketful of business cards or preplaced pieces of paper with your e-mail address on them, give him one with laid-back confidence, and say, "It was nice to meet you (*his name here*)."

5. Now smile and walk away; your work is done. Add him to your Mantris Graph as a Quarter Man. Drop any dread or hope that he will contact you and move on.

This method yields a high rate of return and very little stress. As you get more comfortable with it, feel free to improvise. Just always keep it direct and end it with a way for him to contact you or vice versa.

Guidelines for Collecting Quarters

You are NOT looking for a friend. You are always a woman and he is always a man. This is simply a mind-set; it's not an obvious sexual thing, just an intention.

Always be yourself. Don't pretend you've read the book he's reading or that you play tennis if he's holding a racket. You can be interested; just don't change who you are.

Broaden your horizons. Don't be too choosy. Don't limit your search to your "type." Resist the urge to measure him with your Expectations List or your Deal-Breaker List. You're looking for anyone who seems honest, willing, and loving and single, single, single.

Take the pressure off. You're not walking up to your future husband, just someone to add to your Mantris Graph. Make your goal a full Mantris Graph instead of your baby-daddy and you'll be taking in Quarters like a pinball machine.

When practicing The 4MP, you are out there to collect Quarters. When you are not leading with your ring finger and your fallopian tubes, men will sense the difference in your approach and so will you. In the forest of dating, you're a bold bunny coming in for a sniff, not a bloodthirsty hunter with a shotgun and a bear trap.

Plus, my ambitious 4MPlanners, there's no time to be coy or play games. We've got math to do, and you can't do that without the numbers.

The Internet Connection

The Internet is the 4MPlanner's BEST FRIEND! First off, there is www.thefourmanplan.com. Here you can get info and advice, or bitch and dish with your fellow 4MPlanners. It is your home to discuss all things 4MP.

Second, dating Web sites provide the men you need to fill your Mantris Graph. There are tons of eligible men online looking for love. For those of you who have tried online dating sites and found yourself overwhelmed, The 4MP provides the structure to help you wade through the numbers and the chaos.

> **Hey, what about all those online predators?**
> They exist just as they do in real life. At least online you get a peek into what they have to say for themselves and view it objectively. In person, we are often blinded by the white-hot light of sexual attraction and the effects of two appletinis. Get online and sign up.

Here's how to work the Internet connection:

Create a new e-mail address just for Plan Men: This will help you keep a clean record and do The Plan on your terms. Then someday you can give your grandkids a crazy, futuristic holographic data log about how you met Grandpa back when you had to type your thoughts.

If you are placing an ad: Do not write in innuendos. Keep it squeaky clean and light. Keep the picture above the jugs; let them see your eyes, and wear some clothes. No sexy stuff. Suggestive clothing or language is a green light for those men looking for sex only.

If you are responding to an ad: Read it carefully. You must suspect that they are honest, loving, and willing. Listen to your intuition with regard to their intentions. The words people choose can speak volumes about their character.

Retool your ad and profile every couple of weeks: As you progress in The Plan, you will grow and change. Reworking your ad can steadily reflect that change and attract different types of men every time you reword it. Post new pictures, too—even your face will radiate the new you.

Meet face-to-face: Don't go down the primrose path of falling in love through iChat. Find someone you are interested in and move steadily toward setting up a date. A man living inside your BlackBerry, no matter how spectacular his texting abilities, makes for a lousy dinner companion.

If the man lives out of town: Never go to him unless you have friends, family, or at least one other valid reason for going to that town. (And I mean VALID, not the 3rd Annual Garlic Festival.) If he wants to participate, let him come to you, but NEVER let him stay with you until he is a Three and a Half Man. (More on him later.)

> **Out-of-Towner Downer**
>
> **NOTE:** Because successful long-distance relationships are against the odds, any Plan Man who lives out of town must be handicapped a Quarter of a Man. So if he is a Half Man he only counts as a Quarter, a Whole Man is Three Quarter, and so on.
>
> *A 4MPlanner is allowed only one Out-of-Towner in her Mantris Graph at any one time.*
>
> If you haven't met him in person yet AND he lives out of town, he does not qualify as a Plan Man. Don't give him even a corner of a square. Talk is cheap, but typing is a free ride. Hey, we're looking for the real thing, right? Don't spend too much time on a fantasy built out of 1s and 0s.

Chemistry Shmemistry

Here's a big one that often holds girls back:

"He's sweet, but there's just no chance of a future because there isn't any CHEMISTRY."

Ladies, I'm here to tell you, that's a pile of donkey doo.

Now, I'm not saying that chemistry isn't a wonderful thing, and ultimately a necessary thing between two lovers. But what isn't common knowledge is that chemistry is not necessarily immediate or continuous. Given the right circumstances, it can appear where it was previously absent. Given the wrong circumstances, it can vanish where it was previously dominant.

If:

    A. your past requirement for dating someone is that your loins catch fire when you meet them . . .

And:

    B. you've recently copped to the fact that you suck at love . . .

Then:

    C. you've probably spent most of your romantic life dealing with:

        1. shitheads

        2. assholes

        3. cowards

The guys that we find instantly attractive are often the worst possible choice for a girl who wants to move away from a life fraught with anxiety, drama, and pain. It's entirely possible that your picker is off and that alone is the root of your problems.

Chemistry, like a good stew, can be very effectively created on a low heat setting with lots of eclectic ingredients allowed to mingle together over a long period of time. Sample it too early and it may just taste like a hard rutabaga in dirty water. YUCK! But wait till it's cooked properly and it will be a unique, nutritious, and complex bellyful of melt-in-your-mouth goodness.

The Half Man

The Half Man is a juicy morsel. You've made it past the required second date (see **The Two-Date Minimum,** page 121) and are mutually interested enough to go on a third.

Any man who makes it to a third date automatically becomes a **Half Man.**

> REQUIREMENT: A Plan Man must know that you are dating other men during or before your third date.

In order for The Plan to work, every Plan Man has to know that he is competing with other Plan Men. This refers back to Postulate #2, The Disney Theorem, which states: When it comes to competing for love, there is a big difference between boys and girls. It is only when men start becoming Halves that the real fun of The Plan begins.

Women in general, but particularly those who suck at love, have the tendency to infer their relationship status with a man by watching the behavior and surroundings of their intended. A healthy woman might get her information by looking for a wedding band on his finger, waiting for him to talk about taking the relationship further, watching the way she is treated, if he makes her feel special, if he returns her affections, and so on. The more damaged you are, the keener your senses. For example, I'd listen for their tone or hesitation when they said the words "busy" and "with a friend." I would count wineglasses in the dish rack and scan pillows for long hairs. Oh, I took it deep.

When given the opportunity, men are equipped with the same skill, but they use it the way a racehorse senses a rival horse coming up on the outside. It becomes a sporting and gaming tool that they are quick to employ.

Are there flowers from someone else in your apartment when they come to pick you up?

Are you free on Saturday night?

Are you "tired" on your date because you were "out late" the night before?

I recommend you do the deed of halving a Plan Man sometime during your SECOND DATE. Even if he's the only man in your Graph. It is your *intention* to date others that is the important tidbit of information. Why is during the date or even the beginning of the date the best time to halve a man? Because if you wait until the end of the date, he may mistake it as a kiss-off. If you wait until the third date, the pressure of the deadline may cloud your mojo.

Why do I need to halve them by the third date?

Our culture has deemed the third date the "sex date." I'm not sure who started that one, but if you are using The Wait for Sex Index, you know that three dates may be too early. By telling a Plan Man you are seeing other people, you are also giving the signal that you might hold out on sex until you are seeing him exclusively. By the fourth date, people are getting more emotionally invested. It starts to feel couple-y, and if a Plan Man finds out that late that you are seeing other men, he is more likely to feel a little betrayed and not special. Prior to or during the third date is still a "getting to know you process" and he is unlikely to have developed any possessiveness at that point.

It will only get harder to tell a guy later, especially if you like him, and you may end up losing him instead of getting the opportunity to watch him blossom while he competes to win your affection. Plus, that way you won't be a lying whore.

Half Man Visuals

= the $\frac{1}{2}$ Man

OR

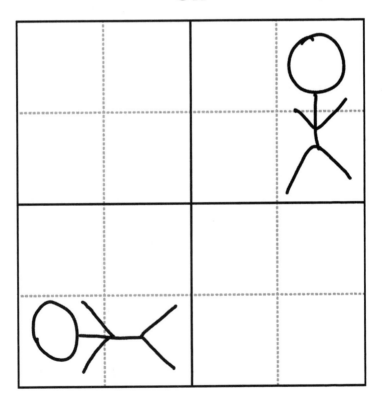

How to Halve a Man

Okay, now you know you have to officially make a Plan Man a Half Man by the end of the third date by letting him know you are seeing other men. At first, this may seem like a very daunting task. But truly, it's not. After you see the effect it has, by the third or fourth time you do it, it will be completely natural. Here are a few sample scripts that are VERY EASY to slip into regular conversation. The best timing for these is before the midpoint of the date. That way he won't misread it as some sissy way of blowing him off.

Sample Scripts

1. "I'm having so much fun dating and you are the _____ guy I'm seeing!"

   Fill in the blank with a word that is TRUE about him—for example: funnest, funniest, cutest, sweetest, most thoughtful, most handsome, most generous, most talented, etc.

   You can say this in response to an act of kindness, cuteness, talent, or anything else that gets you moony-eyed.

   This script not only gives him the information he needs, it also compliments him. It may take him a minute, but he'll get the picture. Trust me.

2. "I'm having so much fun dating. And you're my favorite!"

3. "Who knew a girl could find so many great guys on the Internet!"

Let it roll off. Let him know you are dating multiple men because it's FUN FOR YOU. This changes the very nature of dating.

Letting guys know they are competing is NOT a heavy sit-down talk. KEEP IT LIGHT! Slip it into normal conversation.

The Whole Man

The Whole Man is the real deal. Whole Men know they are competing, and they are staying in the game.

> **A Plan Man qualifies as a Whole Man in one of two ways:**
>
> 1. Physical intimacy past a long kiss good night but still kept over the clothes and at a ninety-degree angle (seated) or vertical with four feet on the floor. For example, you can have a heavy-petting session with the groping kept OVER the bra, but *no dry humping.*
>
> 2. The vocalization of the "L" word—yes, LOVE—by *any* Plan Man.

"LOVE?" you say. And he's only a Whole Man? Aren't you supposed to *consider marrying* the man who says he loves you? What I discovered in my application of The 4MP was that men in competition will do and say things out of their comfort zone to get ahead. Saying "I love being with you" and even "I love you" starts to roll off many a tongue, mostly because it is still easier to SAY love than to DO love.

So don't let your heart go all aflutter because it took you ten months of pleading and dozens of porn-star-like performances to hear it the last time. If hearing "I love you" was your previous goal line, let's bump up the stakes. We're looking for an HONEST, LOVING, and WILLING man who makes your toes curl and treats you like a goddess. So if he says those magic little words, just take it in stride and "accept" his gesture, and if the spirit moves you, return it. Poof, he's now a Whole Man. (It doesn't count if you mention the "L" word first. See "The Talk Paradox," page 125.)

Feel free to allow yourself to open up to love in its many forms, feelings, actions, and words. There is no loss in loving. I do not believe in withholding it and saving it for The Big One. Love is the ability to wish someone happiness and to establish a caring relationship. Each time you love in this way, you plant a seed, and every seed is different. It may be a fruit you have never seen or tasted before. You can tend to a whole garden of love with the sole intention that you might learn to be a better gardener. There is no shame in a seasonal love.

Should a man make it to Whole Man status on the first date or even upon first meeting (hey, I've been drunk at a club, I know it happens), you must give him the honors received by the Quarter Man, which is a way to contact you, and the Half Man, which is to let him know you are seeing other men.

The Whole Man is in a powerful position. If you really see potential with a guy, keep him a Whole Man for as long as possible before promoting him to the next category. In other words, take advantage of The Wait for Sex Index.

Whole Man Visuals

 = 1 Whole Man

OR

How to Keep Them WHOLE

So what if a Plan Man is pressuring you for sex?

It comes down to an energy thing. Let's imagine a man who finds himself lucky enough to be on a date with, say, a MOVIE STAR or the Princess of Morocco. He would have a hard time even trying to kiss her, much less sleep with her. Why? Because her energy is too big, too special. He is in awe of her and, therefore, respectful. He'll still *want* to bang her. But he will not feel entitled to insist until he's really earned it and he's pretty sure that is what she wants, too. It doesn't make her any less sexy or desirable.

Participating in the various steps of The Plan will help you build your energy from where it is now to your fullest potential. Our goal is for you to walk into a room and make men weak in the knees. They wouldn't dare approach you for sex until your intimacy level and their actions have warranted it. Projecting that "star power" will make it easier for men to behave appropriately around you. They will know you're not that girl who throws her ankles behind her knees just to say, "Do you like me?" You're special, and just a sideways glance and a small smile says, "You should be so lucky." Keep that in mind when you're trying to keep a man Whole, and nothing more, just yet.

The Two and a Quarter Man

Okay, here's where you get your groove on. Because of the **Rule of Chuck** (see page 62), it's critical that you not sleep with more than one man at a time.

> Any Plan Man you have sex with becomes a **Two and a Quarter Man.** That way if you are sleeping with two guys, that would add up to four and a half, and that would be too many. Get it?

This category of Plan Man was created because I was in my late twenties to early thirties when I was doing The Plan, and boy, that biological-clock thing is for real. I wanted it all the time. We, too, are slaves to a biological imperative. Once the driving force of physical arousal started coming down the track when I was in my thirties and single, it was like a bullet train. The only way to keep me from mauling a man was to know that I could get it somewhere else. Sadly, as any married gal will tell you, nothing cools our jets like easy access to sex.

As you will see in my Application of The Plan, I used the 2¼ position to hold on to men with whom sex was our best and sometimes only subject. These actually turned out to be the guys I originally thought were "my type" because they would set off the demented Daddy Quester that was attached to my inner thighs. Nevertheless, these were the guys I was hot for.

By having the slot filled (oy, pun alert) by my previous type, I was able to compare apples to oranges (Whole Men to Two and a Quarters) on a weekly basis side by side. It was through this process that I noticed that "my type" tended not to hold up so well in the loving and honest and willing department.

The other way men find themselves in this category is through steady promotion. They have honorably risen up from the unlikely Quarter Man all the way to the top of the heap. They have used The Wait for Sex Index to their advantage and won your heart and your panties. You really like this guy, and you feel like it is time to shine the rest. But wait.

Wait . . .

It's coming. . . .

Two and a Quarter Visual

The $2\frac{1}{4}$ Man

OR

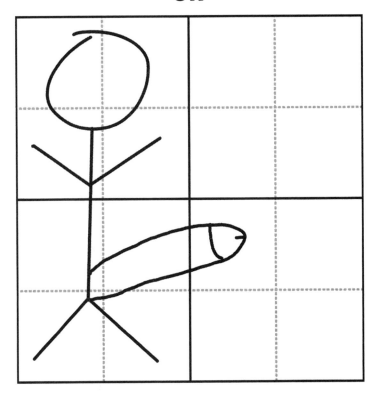

The Slide Rule of Intimacy

The previous distinctions between Plan Men are based on a particular prototype of the 4MPlanner. Female, 20s–60s. Sexually active, no particular religious doctrine, raised with primarily American cultural influences and a strong desire to find THE ONE. Of course, these criteria do not apply to everyone who can use The Plan effectively, as I found out when I was asked by a young Mormon woman, "What if you're waiting until marriage to have sex?" And what about my gal who wrote me from Kenya, where safe sex means no sex? And there's also my darling fifteen-year-old 4MPlanner who is not ready to have sex, she just wants boys to treat her with more respect.

Every woman has different boundaries. Different things that hook her into a man. The Slide Rule of Intimacy gives you a chance to create your own definition of a 2¼. **Basically, your 2¼ boundary is whatever makes you start to develop expectations with a man.** MOST WOMEN cannot have sex without developing some sort of expectation. The 4MPlanner is often relieved of this by using the category of a 2¼ and The Plan to her advantage by dividing her expectations among her various Plan Men. Nonetheless, math alone cannot stave off the demands of the heart.

The SLIDE RULE OF INTIMACY is designed to allow you to examine how each level of physical intimacy hooks you emotionally and thus determines your 2¼. So play with it and see what clicks for you.

Slide Rule of Intimacy

PHYSICAL

Friendly Touch

Hand
Holding

Kissing

Heavy
Petting

Sex

EMOTIONAL

No-Likey

Indifference

Curiosity

Excitement

Expectation

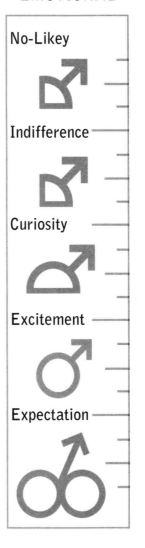

Before I started doing The Plan, my usual M.O. was to get physical first and deal with the emotions it led to later. As a result, I would suddenly find myself having expectations of a man I would have been less than indifferent about simply because I had sex with him. Thereby leading to obsessing over a guy I wasn't even sure I liked! Maddening. Now I know I was best off when the markers on my rulers were even.

Your Slide Rule may have shifted at various points in your dating career, or it may change hourly based on how many cocktails you've had. If you're looking to do The Plan, I recommend keeping the rulers as diagrammed. Or, if you're really looking to hold out, bump the Emotional Ruler up a notch or two.

The Ex Reflex

Ah, the mess o' Exes, a seemingly useless pile of mistakes and heartache: noncommittal, immature bad boys, ineffectual goofballs, and those that fled the Good Ship Clings-A-Lot. But by George, not only is the 4MPlanner gracious, fabulous, and open-minded, she recycles!

Amazing things happen when you start The Plan. One is that a broadcast gets sent through the ether and lights upon those spirits you have loved and lost. Without provocation you may be mysteriously contacted by Exes far and wide. Or you may want to use your newfound skills and attitude to reintroduce yourself to someone who previously fell away for whatever reason. What to do?

Exes can be *grandfathered* into your Mantris Graph. A heebie-jeebie but accurate term since they are exempt from the principles of The Plan that might otherwise keep them out of your Graph.

This allowance can help you autopsy your errors with a new kind of precision. It can allow you to compare the old with the new and see how your tastes and perceptions have changed. It can bring closure and maturity to what may have been an ugly breakup. It can even reunite two people who were meant to be together had not one or both of them sucked at love so badly.

Also, let's not ignore the fact that it's a great source for an easy Two and a Quarter.

An Ex gets only one time around as a Plan Man, one spin around The Graph. Once an Ex is in your Mantris, he must be considered by all the principles and compete fairly with the other Plan Men. If he gets the boot again, he's out for good.

How to Use the Mantris

If you have one Plan Man of each value, you have achieved a Perfect Full Mantris! Your Mantris Graph would look like this:

Or let's say you go speed dating and meet sixteen men with whom you exchange phone numbers or e-mail addresses. You have achieved a Full Mantris, and it will look like this:

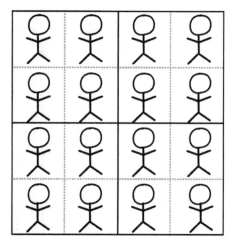

Or if you are The Bachelorette going on four hometown dates, your Full Mantris would look like this:

Or if you are Snow White living with seven dwarfs with a crush on you, your nearly full Mantris looks like this:

Which still leaves space for you to meet your prince. However it organically occurs for you is right.

9. THE PRINCIPLES OF THE 4MP

Principle: *n.* 1. a standard used for decision making

2. a predetermined policy or mode of action

The following Principles are the tools a 4MPlanner uses to move forward through The Plan with consistency and integrity.

"Three Rules of Work:
Out of clutter find simplicity.
From discord find harmony.
In the middle of difficulty lies opportunity."

—ALBERT EINSTEIN

Principles of The 4MP

These six principles are designed to help a 4MPlanner re-move moral and emotional ambiguity. Things like:

"What will I do if this yo-yo asks me for a second date?"

"Did I freak Dreamboat out when I said that I want our kids to have his nose?"

"How am I supposed to have a meaningful relationship with my boss if his wife keeps interrupting us?"

These dilemmas take up a hell of a lot of a girl's time.

Because your execution of The Plan requires you to spend more time looking for, talking to, and dating men, fol-lowing these principles will help you spend less time wonder-ing about, waiting on, and judging men. These principles are here to guide you as your Plan Men step out of your Graph and you start to experience them with all the complications that arise out of human interaction.

The Yes Factor

> **Principle #1:** Say YES to every invitation.

Your objective is to fill The Mantris Graph and keep it full. **If you are invited to a party, an art exhibit, a rodeo, or a monster truck rally, you say YES. If a friend offers to set you up, or your aunt Gladys wants you to meet her dentist, or that odd little man from Accounting asks you out, regardless of your "opinion" of them, you say YES. Why?**

Four major reasons:

1. So that you will sample from a larger pool of specimens and not just choose men you are attracted to, because so far that has gotten you bubkes.
2. So that if you like one man A LOT, you will not break out your Laser Beam and Death Claws or inappropriately poke him with your ring finger and fallopian tubes because you will be otherwise distracted.
3. So that you don't have to FAKE playing hard to get, or fake feeling fabulous and desirable, or fake being gracious and compassionate. It will all simply be true.
4. Because The Four Man Plan is a numbers game. The more tickets you buy, the better chance you have of winning!

*Exceptions to **The Yes Factor** are **The Chick's Chick Angle** (page 117) and **The Breakup Ladder** (page 131).*

The Yes Factor

The Chick's Chick Angle

There are two kinds of women in this world: Chick's Chicks and Dick's Chicks.

Let's say you're meeting a delicious man—let's call him Dick—for the first time and in your conversation he asks you,

"Can I buy you a drink?"

Hmm, promising. But then you notice a wedding ring.

If you're a **Chick's Chick** you *lean back, thereby creating the Chick's Chick Angle,* and say "No, thank you."

If you're a **Dick's Chick** you lean forward and say, "Sure."

He starts to get comfortable with you, he sees you have noticed his ring, so he explains,

"My wife and I are having problems."

A Chick's Chick gives him the "whatever" head tilt and discourages him from going any further.

A Dick's Chick displays compassion and sympathy and perhaps even gives Dick an arm touch and coos, "You poor thing."

He persists with, *"She just doesn't seem to get that I have needs."*

The Dick's Chick says, "That bitch just doesn't understand you."

A Chick's Chick tells him, "Perhaps you should be telling *her* this, bring her some flowers and unload the dishwasher, and maybe THEN she'd want to have sex with you." TA DA!

The Chick's Chick Angle

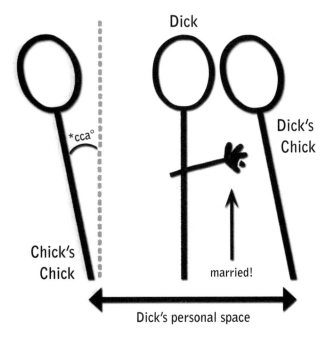

*abbreviation of chick's chick angle

As a Chick's Chick, you get on THE WOMAN'S SIDE. *Always.* Behave as if it were your best friend's husband hitting on you, as if you know her whole story, because you do. Of course she isn't blameless, and he may have a legitimate gripe and they may be headed for divorce or breakup. But if they are still together, then it is not your business. Talking to a stranger rather than to his woman, a friend, or a therapist is a coward's move. So stand up for her, advocate her side of the story, and pretend it's you waiting for him at home while he looks outside for sympathy.

Go with the very probable odds that he needs to work his poop out with her (even if she's a crazy bitch and COMPLETELY at fault) before he would do anything right by you. If we all supported that faceless woman on the other side of that yummy man instead of falling for the biggest sucker bet in the world, the romantic landscape would be a much safer place for us all.

If that isn't motivation enough, here's the real secret: Every woman, upon birth, is issued one superpowerful voodoo spell. Most will not choose to use it, or even know they have it, unless provoked. When a woman finds out she's been cheated on, regardless of who is to blame, who started it, or who did what when, she will without hesitation hurl that voodoo toward her lover and the other woman. She will sit in deep concentration wishing the worst possible fate on all parties involved. If you have ever been that betrayed, as I have, you know what I'm talking about. And whether the parties involved would regret it in the future or not, that voodoo curse almost always works. One need only browse the tabloid rags and read the fates of those who choose to steal unavailable men to confirm this theory.

I, myself, am a reformed Dick's Chick. I lost my virginity to a cook where I used to wait tables. We tried to keep it secret from our boss—not only because fraternizing was frowned upon at our restaurant, but because she was his fiancée. She found out. Voodoo was cast.

My punishment? I was fired and got a nasty bladder infection. His punishment? He still had to marry that nasty witch and have her lord the incident over him for all their wedded days. If you've ever been a Dick's Chick, you can change teams at any time. Now would be fine.

Be a Chick's Chick. Maintain the angle.

The Two-Date Minimum, or Give Pete a Chance

> **Principle #3:** To examine each specimen, you will need a control sample and a test sample. Therefore, The Plan requires a minimum of two dates per Plan Man, whether you like him or not.

Ohmigawd, WHY!?

Four reasons:

1. This principle is about collecting data. We like to think that we have an amazing capacity to read people through first impressions. Even if you are excellent at it in other areas of your life, we must refer back to Postulate #5: You Suck at Love.

2. Some of the most HONEST, LOVING, and WILLING men make a terrible first impression. Probably because they just don't get as much practice as Pietro Suavo, certified hot guy.

3. Of the happily married women I have talked to, half of them confess to not liking their husband upon first meeting him. You heard me, HALF! He was not their type, he was strictly "friend material," he did something stupid on their first date, or he straight up bugged the shit out of them. But for some reason, they gave him another chance—and ended up falling in love with and marrying the doofus.

Two-Date-Minimum Flow Chart

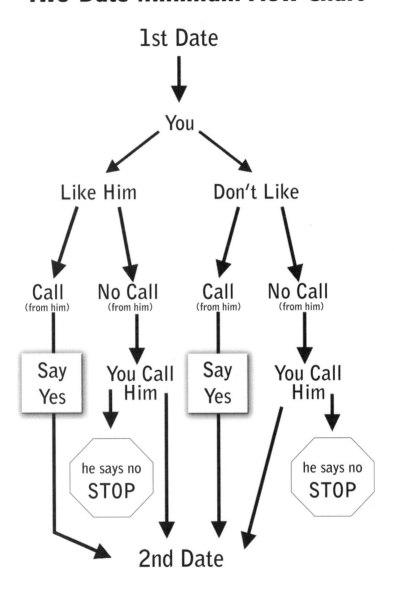

4. On first dates, people often exhibit erratic behavior out of nervousness, or they play it safe, covering up their true selves to appear "normal." With each man, you need to suss out his true behavior patterns.

Buck up and accept that if you are going on a first date, there will be a second date whether you like him or not. So cancel your girlfriend's standing order for the forty-five-minutes-into-the-first-date "emergency" phone call.

This principle also serves to disable your relentless first-date function, The Constant Judger. You will not get to spend your first date racking up all the reasons why you will never go out with him again and trying to figure out how to exit as quickly as possible. Instead, you will automatically start looking for something you like about him so that you can stand the idea of going out with him again.

Who's Pete? Pete and I met through a personals ad and we hit it off right away on the phone. Upon our first meeting, he was flustered; I guess I had forgotten to mention the fact that I was Chinese, and he blurted out, "Oh, I didn't know you were *Oriental*." Sigh. That could have been enough for me to turn on my heel and exit. But I stayed through a pleasant meal during which he intermittently apologized for his comment and shock. I kept telling him it was fine, but he finally went so far as to remove his shoe and hold it over the dinner table, *while our food was on it,* to show me that his shoe was Made in China to prove to me that he was not a racist. Oooh, nooo.

But based on my commitment to The Two-Date Minimum, we did go out again. And on our next date, he noticed my knees, slightly ravaged by a Rollerblading Incident, and with that same lack of censorship he said, "God, I love a woman with scarred-up knees." Uh-oh. And then: "It really shows that she's not afraid to go out there and live life." Rock on, Shoe Boy! This awkward blurt-out has served to make me far less self-conscious—nay, proud of my frequently skinned and permanently scarred knees. His big unedited mouth turned out to be an endearing quality. Marry him, I did not. But grateful to him, I am. Thanks for Date #2, Pete.

Looking for the best in someone is a great thing to practice and makes you a more pleasant date well worth the price of a sushi dinner. Furthermore, because of the validation that inherently comes from accepting or pursuing a second date, you will both be more comfortable and yourselves the next time you hang out. Validation is as pleasurable to give as to receive. Validation is a form of intimate, unconditional, and universal love that you can leave your knickers on for.

So even if they do not call you, seven days after your date it's your responsibility to call them and ask them if they would like to go out again. Only if they reject the second date are you allowed to skip this principle with a Plan Man, remove him from your Mantris Graph, and collect a replacement.

The Talk Paradox

Principle #4: Initiate conversation,
but do not initiate "The Talk."

A 4MPlanner is not afraid to approach a man. She initiates conversation and sparkles when necessary. On dates, she reveals herself and is curious about others.

However, the following statements or anything hinting around these statements are forbidden during The Plan:

"Where do you see this going?"

"How do you feel about us?"

"Are you ready for commitment, marriage, babies, a mortgage, college funds, etc.?"

We women tend to ask these questions WAY TOO EARLY and at a time when, most likely, the man hasn't even thought about them yet. This conversation train scares the bejeezus out of them when introduced prematurely. The best way to avoid talking about these things too soon is to wait until HE'S ready. Your fantasies about your imaginary future with him or your complaints about his peccadillos and how they might interfere with his fathering abilities must stay between you, your girlfriends, your shrink, and your journal.

The Talk Paradox

"If A equals success, then the formula is:
A = X + Y + Z.
X is work. Y is play.
Z is keep your mouth shut."

—ALBERT EINSTEIN

The less time you spend talking about your relationship, the more time you'll spend actually having one.

Part of this principle is to let The Plan Men discover their answers to these questions on their own. And, would you believe, ask YOU these questions. If a Plan Man does initiate such talk, by all means answer him honestly with your big loving heart. This step will become very important when we get to the crown jewel of men, The Three and a Half Man.

Hit the brakes on "The Talk." Let them start it.

Lu's Pendulum

Principle #5: While you are getting the hang of The Plan, an act that is perceived as "good" by Plan standards may be followed by an act perceived as "bad."

There is a reason that workouts are often followed by hot-fudge sundaes, and well-met deadlines are often followed by the misuse of sick days.

The thrust of Lu's Pendulum is this: When you are following the principles of The Plan that do not as yet feel natural to you, don't be surprised if you have an adverse reaction. For example, you may feel forced to go on a pleasant second date with someone "sweet" but not your cup of tea one night, and therefore allow yourself to have raunchy, drunken sex with your alcoholic ex the next. You may be gracious while your favorite Plan Man drops out one day, and send a gay stripper to his office the next.

Until something like the Chick's Chick Angle becomes your natural response due to your own sense of integrity, not something imposed on you by *some book* written by *some girl* who's *not even a doctor,* you will most likely act out. It's cool—just keep checking in with yourself and try to do what makes you, your deepest authentic you, feel centered.

The key is to not think that you deserve a trophy for doing something that deep down you know is right anyway, like giving a nice but uni-browed guy a chance or not making out with your roommate's boyfriend. And at the same time, don't berate yourself for a slipup, like showing a guy your wedding-planning book on a first date or skipping out on a mandatory second date. If you know you are acting on your true integrity, do a little dance and move on; if you mess up, examine your reasons and pick up where you left off. Don't give up because you slip up. Don't go back to a pack-a-day habit just because you had one little cigarette in a moment of stress. Get back with the program, because you know in the end it's in your best interest. Humility and forgiveness are two great things to practice on yourself, and they will get you that much closer to attracting a partner who knows how to do the same.

What if I mess up bad?

The Four Man Plan is meant to give you a set of guidelines to measure yourself against. There is no 4MP Police and it is not necessary to always follow it to the letter to get results. After a while, the more natural The Plan starts to feel, the less erratic the swing becomes. Eventually, the swinging pendulum stops being a stomach-dropping roller-coaster ride and eases into the peaceful rhythm of your continued growth.

Lu's Pendulum

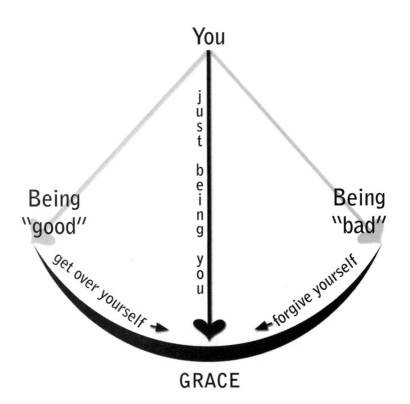

You

just being you

Being "good"

Being "bad"

get over yourself →

← forgive yourself

GRACE

The Breakup Ladder

> **Principle #6:** Breaking up with a Plan Man
> is not up to you.

Breaking up with or dismissing someone because you feel "there's no chemistry" or to "spare their feelings" or because you "don't see it going anywhere" is not allowed. There are only five reasons to break it off with a Plan Man:

1. They give you The Ickies.

Use your intuition—it's your first line of defense. For those of us whose intuition may be a little inaccurate when it comes to matters of the heart (you suck at love), here are some guidelines. The Ickies would include:

a. **That very specific feeling where they make you feel bad about yourself somehow.** (*This does not include feeling like you are a mean person because you might squash this nice guy like a bug.*) Did they somehow discourage or belittle you? Did they cruise other women and think you didn't notice? Did they make you feel like a side of beef?

b. **They manage to treat you like crap and then make you feel guilty about it.** This is a subtle tactic of an abuser. It's your classic "Look what you made me do!" Run!

c. **They clearly are not honest, loving, or willing.**
   - Not honest = liars. However, do not waste any time being suspicious. Always assume you are being told the truth. Liars do not hold up well in competition against honest men and will usually naturally weed themselves out of The Plan.
   - Not loving = pricks. Again, so much easier to spot in competition. Standing alone, these can be the rather attractive "bad boy" types.
   - Not willing = close-minded, inflexible, uncomfortable with new things and new ideas, need-to-have-things-done-on-their-terms jerkwads. Long-term, you're gonna hate this guy no matter how good he looks on paper.

d. **Generation gap.** If it exceeds fifteen years in either direction, you could consider it The Ickies OR NOT. Age is a function of attitude and lifestyle, and these days there are boys in sixty-year-old bodies and extremely savvy teenagers. So I'll leave this one up to you. If you are living in different worlds maturity-wise, you can choose to negate The Yes Factor because of it. But don't rule anyone out simply because of a number. Not age, salary, or zip code. Okay, maybe a prison ID number, but that's it!

e. **They make you fear for your safety.** Definitely try new stuff, but don't do anything that you feel would put you in harm's way. Use your spidey senses and keep yourself safe.

What is NOT The Ickies:
The sick feeling you get because he has a receding hairline, wears pleated pants, or mispronounces your favorite wine. That's just you being a poopyhead.

If you are not sure if a Plan Man qualifies for The Ickies or not, you must adhere to **The Two-Date Minimum.**

If you ARE sure he qualifies for The Ickies and you still want to keep him around, go for it. You may have one bona fide Ickmeister in your Graph at any given time. In reality, those who suck at love often LOVE THE ICKIES. It is exciting and comforting and weirdly familiar. Sure, I get it. There's something really great about going out with someone who just can't get his shit together. *Because then you get to be the better person.* And when you're the better person, you get to work on their shit, not yours. Aah, much easier.

Also, if The Ickies happen to be your type, leaving one in your Mantris helps you do direct comparisons. It's a powerful learning tool. That is, you will feel much more powerful when you finally learn that he is a tool.

2. They Drop Out on their own.

Oy, this can be heartbreaking. But you'd be surprised how doing The 4MP can help soften this blow. Losing a dish off a buffet is a lot easier to take than burning a prime-rib roast. You cannot pursue a dropout Plan Man except for the one-time Two-Date Minimum phone call. A 4MPlanner does not chase, does not beg, does not stalk. You cannot retort with vengeful e-mails or whiny voice mails. There just isn't time or energy to waste.

A dropout Plan Man can, however, reenter The Plan of his own volition. If he asks to return and you have room in your Graph, you may accept him. You get to decide his new value and demote him if necessary (see page 138).

3. They are Squeezed Out of The Plan for lack of space.

Let's say you are such a great 4MPlanner that you have achieved a full Mantris Graph. You may squeeze out the Plan Man of your choice to make room for a new Plan Man. So if you really want to get rid of someone, break out The Methods of Collection and The Yes Factor and squeeze them out. Previously squeezed out men may return at your request or if they make another play for you at a later date when you have room in your Mantris.

4. Your new 2¼ "Chucks Out" your old 2¼.

Huh? Let me explain: Let's say you go out with Bobby, your favorite Whole Man, and you sleep with him. The next night you meet Jimmy and, oops, you sleep with him, too. Then Bobby must be Chucked Out of your Mantris Graph NEVER TO RETURN.

Yes, that's right; not only can you sleep with only one

Plan Man at a time, but if he *was* your Two and a Quarter, and someone else gets promoted to Two and a Quarter, then the previous Plan Man must be removed from the box, **never to return. He cannot be simply demoted, he's OUT. FOREVER.**

Let me say this another way: Don't sleep with Man #1, then sleep with Man #2 thinking that you'll go back to sleeping with Man #1 on your next date with him. NO. NO. NO. The new Two and a Quarter Man eliminates ALL men you have ever slept with before him. **So chuck them out wisely.**

WHY? Here's where I get bossy boots for a minute: Because The Four Man Plan is about (1) getting and keeping respect, from men and from yourself, and (2) forward progress. So if you could switch your Two and a Quarters back and forth, there is nothing to prevent you from sleeping with several different men willy-nilly. This would create lots of drama, make you confused, and get you emotionally entangled with men who aren't going to want a monogamous relationship with you anyway because they figure you're a girl who's all about the sex and that puts us right back where we started.

Any man you have slept with and then overthrown to sleep with someone else is not someone you really have a chance at a long-term relationship with. WHY NOT? Because good men, men like Chuck, find it hurtful, distasteful, disrespectful, and ultimately a blow to male pride that you would want anyone else after you have been with them. In their minds, they made you pure by having sex with you and now you've gone and sullied yourself again. Penis Cooties, remember?

What about Threesomes and Orgies?

If you've been harboring fantasies about them and you are still single, I highly recommend you go for it. Don't wait until you're five years into a relationship and then slap your head and say, "I never got to have a threesome!" Because then it is just TOO LATE. If the opportunity presents itself and no one is going to get hurt, have at it. Just know that those two other people, be they guy/guy, guy/girl, whatever, those people are *Chucked Out* as soon as the lights come on. Trust me, you're not going to want to have breakfast with these people, much less attempt a relationship with any of them.

Also, the Chuck Out rule makes you wait and choose to promote a Plan Man to your 2¼ very carefully.

The Four Man Plan is a game of attrition in which pieces are removed from the board when they are outplayed.

5. They are Ineligible.

For example, they are: already in a monogamous relationship, gay, a priest, your eighth-grade student, etc.

Unavailable means unavailable. It should not make him more delicious, it should make him smell like doo-doo.

Breakup Ladder Visual

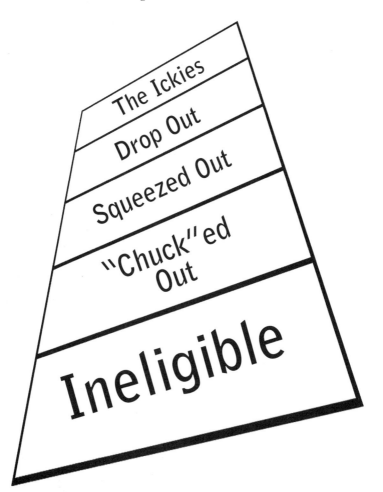

Should He Be SMOTED or DEMOTED?

Just when you thought it was getting complicated:

> *A Plan Man may be reassigned a lesser value without being removed entirely from your Mantris.*

Here are a few scenarios:

A. A Whole Man leaves town for an extended period of time. Bump him to a Half or even a Quarter if he moves permanently.

B. A Plan Man of any value reveals that he is sleeping with someone else, though he insists it is NOT a monogamous relationship. He can be smoted or demoted or stay the same. Do as you please. Coochie Cooties are nearly as bad to women as Penis Cooties are to men. Only you know the level of purity you require for the potential of that particular relationship.

C. You really liked Eduardo and it got *mucho caliente,* so you slept with him, making him your Two and a Quarter. But as it turns out, he doesn't have a lot of time for dating right now. Along comes Harold, who's REALLY SWEET, makes a lot of time for you, doesn't mind taking things slow; he may be the future Mr. You, but oh so *not* your between-the-sheets type. He doesn't mind that you are dating other men, but you are pretty sure he would be crushed to find out you're sleeping with someone else. But dammit, Eduardo is so HOT, you're not ready to chuck him out forever for the sake of Harold's feelings. What to do?

You can DEMOTE Eduardo back to a Whole Man (that means back to over the clothes and ninety-degree angles!), giving him equal status as long as you do not PROMOTE Harold up to a 2¼. If you do, Eduardo is Chucked Out, even from his Whole Man status.

D. Joey was previously your boy toy 2¼ but now you're in deep. You love everything about him except the fact that he's also bedding other women, and this suddenly is not so swell for you. How do you separate yourself from the pack? Continue seeing him, but stop sleeping with him. Explain the situation and demote him back to a Whole Man. Spare your heart and let him know you're special. If removing the option of romping makes him not want to spend time with you, then at least you'll be standing when you find out where you stand.

10. CONCLUDING THE PLAN

Let's not be like the boys and get all excited about a plan and not have an exit strategy.

"Peace cannot be kept by force. It can only be achieved by understanding."

— A.E.

Concluding The Plan

Unsucking at Love is a lifelong pursuit. Just when you think you've got the hang of it, the next level shows itself. It is not unlike Ms. Pacman. You clear a few screens, and then you meet Pacman; you get good at running that course, and then here comes Junior . . . and on and on it goes. You can always beat your own high score.

Doing The Four Man Plan is not intended to be indefinite. I suggest signing on for semesters that last between four and six months. Some 4MPlanners will ace the course on their first go-round, some will repeat it over the summer and a brush up a few years later, and some will just take an equivalence exam.

There are three ways to successfully end The Plan.

Conclusion #1:
Your Ultimate Goal,
The Three and a Half Man

Winner! Winner! Lobster dinner!

This guy has really stuck it out. He has competed with gusto. He has won your heart. He has shown you a connection that you are happy to move into the future with. He makes you feel like the incredible, gorgeous creature that you are, and you are digging who you are when you are with him.

There are five components to The 3½ Man. He is:

1. **HONEST**
2. **LOVING**
3. **WILLING**
4. **He has expressed an earnest interest in a monogamous relationship with you. And you want the same from him.**
5. **You love him.**

He has at least ONE of your original deal-breaker qualities, maybe more, but you are crazy about him anyway.

He is not perfect, but neither are you, and you can express that to each other and feel comfortable. Or, even better, you can both laugh about it.

He shines in comparison with the other Plan Men and makes it easy for you to let go of the rest.

The 3½ Man Venn Diagram

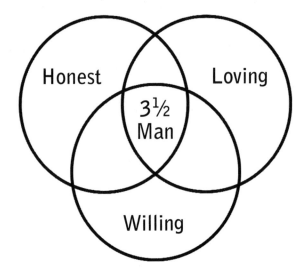

Why is he only Three and a Half and not Four? By now you should have realized that no one man can fulfill all of our needs.

Finding one guy who is Three and a Half is a tall order and should be embraced.

Now it's time for you to release the other men with dignity and end The Plan. Tell the other Plan Men: **"I've really enjoyed your company, but I've decided to be monogamous with one man."** And now you're out, Girl Scout!

> **Be advised:** If things don't work out with Mr. Three and a Half, I suggest you wait at least three months (a season) before starting The Plan again. You will need to reassess, hang out with your girls, and/or book in some therapy before you're ready to whip out The Mantris Graph again.

All that said,

I AM SOOO HAPPY FOR YOU!!

At the end of the day, love is the only game in town.

Conclusion #2:
The Planless Plan, or the Graphectomy

So you've learned a few things and are ready to drop the harried pace of The Mantris Graph and relax. I love it! Maybe you've learned that meeting men is not as hard as you thought and that dating can be a lot of fun. You are no longer obssessive, you've found that you don't mind a pet ferret or a snorting laugher as much as you thought, and you have developed clear boundaries. Fan-friggin'-tastic! Stay a Chick's Chick and keep on searching for that great match for you. Thank you for playing!

Conclusion #3:
Successfully Single

There's a bunch of you that just start doing The Plan to figure something out, heal a squished-on heart, or just prove to yourself that you've still got it. I hope your research unearthed the fact that you are one hot piece of ass with lots to offer this world. It's not time to settle down yet—being single is way too much fun. Fly, be free!

 "Let every man be respected as an individual and no man idolized."

—ALBERT EINSTEIN

11. HOW TO APPLY THE PLAN

How The Four Man Plan worked for me.

"Science is a wonderful thing if one does not have to earn one's living at it."

—ALBERT EINSTEIN

My Application of The 4MP

I started with a young bartender with spectacular abs: **The Ab Man**. I had a hard time getting over my old patterns, and I figured that by the way I had this set up, this might be my last Ab Fuck. So on our second date, he became my 2¼ Man.

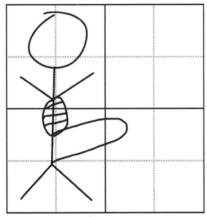

Soon after, I was introduced to a ruggedly handsome romantic whom we'll call **The Marlboro Man**. He was mildly famous, the life of the party, and had plush and rugged hands.

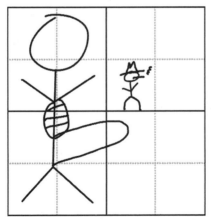

Then **Vishnu** and I connected at a chi gong retreat. The weekend we spent together should have qualified him as a Half Man, but since he suffered from The Out-of-Towner Downer, he stayed a Quarter Man.

I was hanging out in my yard with my dogs when I spotted **Malaka Hiki Hi**. Yes, I actually met a man in my backyard. He was staying at my neighbor's house. **Malaka Hiki Hi** was a Hawaiian hipster who loved to go shopping with me and was so damn likable, he could actually get away with winking at people and pointing at them with gun hands.

The Ab Man soon proved the validity of **The Wait for Sex Index**. By the fifth date, we said nothing, screwed, and afterward I couldn't even get him to walk me to my car. He needed to be Chucked Out. So by order of the Ex Reflex, I brought back **Romeo**, clogs, extra Cindys, and all.

Not too long after, **Malaka Hiki Hi** told me he LOVED me. I thought it was adorable, and I accepted. Bumping him up to a **Whole Man**.

The Marlboro Man passes **Malaka Hiki Hi** in the driveway on his way to pick me up for our third date. They stop, they turn and face each other and shake each other's hand with a gentlemanly bow. After recently finding out he was competing, he proved that chivalry and **The Disney Theorem** were alive and well.

Check it out! Here you see I have a Perfect Full **Mantris**, one of each value, which is all a girl can really handle. But The Graph is a living, breathing organism that continues to delight and surprise.

Vishnu was **Squeezed Out** of The Plan when a girlfriend of mine set me up with **Nick**, who was, God bless him, *a mime*, a previously repellent category of men. But he made me laugh when, to kiss me, he mimed climbing me like a tree.

On my second date with **Nick, Malaka Hiki Hi** popped by. We invite him in for cocktails, and while I'm in the bathroom **Malaka Hiki Hi** *hits on Nick* and is eliminated for being ineligible and also in a bizarre way for not maintaining the Chick's Chick Angle. Not cool.

The **Marlboro Man** seems to genuinely care for me, so I give him a little action and he is promoted to a **Whole Man**.

My dear friend **Danny** has always had a bit of a crush on me. My intention to consider him differently made him a **Quarter Man**. I realized that a man who is interested in you romantically would rather have a fraction of a chance as your love interest than be your best friend forever.

They were all being unbelievably sweet and attentive, and I was becoming a self-confident, self-respecting woman with goddesslike superpowers. The Plan had brought out qualities in me that I didn't know existed. I was compassionate and loving without being a slut. I was in demand and desirable without being a bitch. As a result, I was adored, respected, and sought after. It was fun. But for all of their efforts, I didn't allow anyone to usurp Romeo from his dominant position. Chucking him out meant losing him forever, and none of the other men meant that much to me.

I wasn't sure what the end of this long equation would be. But it certainly wasn't hurting me. So I kept moving forward.

Earl

About five months into The Plan, I met Earl at a restaurant bar. He was completely not my type. I like my men to come in olives and browns, and he was so *pink* and *blue*. But I had room in my Mantris, so I dutifully struck up a conversation with him and asked him what he was eating. He shared his tilapia with me and bought me a Manhattan, and we had a very fun, surprisingly intimate talk. I gave him my phone number.

He called a couple of weeks later, but instead of asking me for a date, he became an energy-healing client of mine. (A subject for an entirely different book.) During our first session, he told me he hadn't cried in about fifteen years even though he felt sad a lot. He was HONEST. During our second session, I had my hands around his heart chakra and I could feel this pure, unconditional love vibrating between us, and it was powerful enough to bring a pool of tears to the porches of his eyes.

We worked together for a dozen sessions. It was intense and tender and challenging for both of us. He was always on time, respectful, and generous. He did every crazy homework assignment I gave him. All the while, he knew about The Plan. He passed Malaka Hiki Hi in the driveway and even had lunch with Romeo and me one day. Watching the conversation between Earl and Romeo allowed me to view them both more objectively than ever before. Seeing them side by side, it struck me how Earl seemed open, calm, and worldly while Romeo was closed off, skeptical, and brooding.

A few weeks before Christmas, Earl and I completed

our work together and decided it would be our last session. It was bittersweet, because we had developed a bit of a bond. As we were saying good-bye, he scooped me up (he'll tell you I jumped up), and when I tried to give him a kiss on the cheek, he turned and gave me a kiss that caught just a bit of our moist inside lips. Then he walked down my long driveway and I didn't know if I would ever see him again.

It was a brief kiss, and considering all the attention I was getting from other Plan Men it shouldn't have affected me, but it did. It put me into a sweat, an emotional, spiritual, sexual heat that I couldn't shake. He was LOVING. I struggled with the moral ambiguity of having feelings for a client. I tried eating, calling girlfriends, calling Plan Men to get my mind off Earl, but I couldn't.

I turned to the I Ching, an ancient Chinese text used for divination, my moral compass and my absolute guide in times of confusion, and I asked, "Who is Earl to me?" as I threw the coins, "Who is Earl to me?" The answer was Hexagram #48, The Source, The Well: **"This hexagram represents the deepest, inexhaustible, divinely centered source of meaning and nourishment from the center of the earth."**

Okay, that's deep. "Well, I have room for Earl," I told myself. "What's he? Maybe another Quarter or Half Man?" I called him. "Um, Earl, since you left I've been having some inappropriate thoughts about you and—"

"I'll be at your place in half an hour," he said, and hung up. He was WILLING.

He arrived with a bottle of wine and a few CDs. I was babbling about how wrong it was for us to get together and then I fell for the oldest trick in the book—Marvin Gaye. Suddenly, we were dancing, and before you know it, we were kissing. Then that weird unconditional love feeling rose up again, and a moment later, a swelling breast was met by an ecstatic hand and Earl became a **Whole Man** his first night on The Plan.

The holidays were a whirlwind of activities with The Plan Men: family parties, office boozefests, and romantic outings. Earl had gone home to Minnesota for Christmas, but he was calling me every day to stay in the game, from church, the mall, really making a long-distance effort. New Year's Eve was fast approaching. And this was not any New Year's Eve, it was 2000 going into 2001, the REAL *New Millennium's Eve,* which made it the Super Bowl of all date nights.

I meditated on what I should do on that night: "Whom should I be with?" And I heard this booming voice say, **"Go east and be with nature."** That is so typical of my internal booming voice. It never just says, "Go to that party with Danny." Nope, it's always got to be cryptic and mysterious and left to interpretation. But it is also never wrong, so I waited to see what the offers were.

Every Plan Man asked me out for a New Year's celebration. I was invited to a party by one and out for a romantic evening by another. The most interesting offer was from The Marlboro Man, to go kayaking in the Channel Islands. Nature! But that was west. And then there was Earl, calling every day from the Midwest. With nieces and nephews screaming in the background, he asked me what *I* wanted to do for New Year's Eve. Clever monkey. I told him, "I'm not sure, but I have to go east and I'm pretty sure I have to be in nature." He said, **"Okay, let's grab what we need to be in nature and drive east."** He won the night, because despite my vagueness, he had faith in me and was so *willing* to make an effort just to be with me.

We spent New Year's Eve day in search of . . . something. We didn't know what, but I knew I would recognize it when I saw it. We cruised overbooked campsites and dingy roadside motels. They just weren't right. After hours of searching, my arm shot straight out. Even I was surprised to see where my finger was aiming: a triangular rock formation with signs indicating that it was illegal to camp there. Earl is more the law-abiding type, but one pleading look from me brought him to the dark side. We stashed the car and camped in a beautiful spot surrounded by the red rocks of Joshua Tree, like the only two people on the surface of our own little planet. Earl pitched our tent, set up our camping kitchen, and then found a spot behind a bush and dug us a toilet. Meanwhile, I made our bed, prepared our dinner, and explored our surroundings. We had made a perfectly protected, fully functional natural home. One of the nicest homes I had ever seen, and a bell went off in my head. *"This guy would make a great husband."*

That night we climbed to the top of a chilly flat rock to watch stars shoot across the sky. There were so many, we stopped counting and started kissing to ring in the New Millennium. And with our hats and our boots on, Earl became my Two and a Quarter Man.

Early in the morning, I snuck away, looked up at the sky, and asked, "What am I supposed to do with this guy?" And with shattering clarity, the booming voice answered, **"Give him five years."**

"What the hell does that mean?" I asked. It didn't reply again. The booming voice does not appreciate my sarcastic retorts.

The next day, on another one of my whims, we went to the Deep Creek Hot Springs. We hiked down to the river, where there were several nude bathers in the various pools. We stripped down and joined them.

We stayed until we were alone, and it was dark. The moon was full. Lying in a shallow pool, I looked up to find Earl holding a bottle of water that he had filled *at the source* of the springs, a hole in the wall that bubbled out hot mineral water from the center of the earth. He knelt down and gently poured it over my hair and my face, then my shoulders and my chest. Wow. I had never felt more pure or nourished. The I Ching and my booming voice were right again.

When we returned, I Chucked Romeo out of The Plan. It was a tender good-bye, and we both cried. He thought we had finally settled on the perfect multipartner relationship, and I knew that I was losing my last great Quest subject. To this day, I can honestly say that I still love him dearly for the lessons he taught me.

After that, The Plan continued, but it seemed as if I was always choosing Earl over the other Plan Men, or that he was always the one who made himself available. He was great at parties, he didn't mind shopping, and he didn't know any other Cindys. He became my best friend.

This went on for about a month when he said, "Cindy, I realize I'm one of four, but I'd really like it if it was just the two of us, because for me, you're the one."

What?! A man suggesting monogamy?

"Really? Why?" I asked.

"Because I love you, An-Pai." And a shy smile played across his face.

Like so many years ago with Chuck, I closed my eyes and took a deep breath.

This time, that peaceful loving feeling settled into my heart and I wasn't barfy at all. I wanted it to be just us, too, and I was ready.

"I love you, too, Earl."

I dropped the other men. I dropped The Plan. This Midwestern boy had come out of nowhere, and with dashing aplomb, he became my Three and a Half Man.

After a few months, I took Earl home to meet my mom.

She looked him up and down, frowning in disbelief. I swear she leaned in for a smell to see if he was for real. And then the verdict: "Ooooooooh, I like Earl. I can tell he's a *good man*. How did you find him?"

"Well, I developed this Plan, and I . . . he, um . . . we, uh . . . just lucky, I guess," I replied.

Four and a half years went by and finally we got engaged. In those years, we bought a house, lost our dear cat to cancer, adopted a third dog, got lots of therapy, and opened up two new businesses. We are teammates and lovers, best friends and co-chefs.

And I loved him to death . . .

Sixty-five percent of the time.

The rest of the time, he drives me FUCKING NUTS.

That "Give him five years" comment rang in my ears. What did that mean?! How could he be my Prince Charming? Those fairy tales never said "and they lived happily ever after TWO-THIRDS of the time!!"

Even so, Earl had never once left my side.

A Wedding on the Beach

Then this really weird thing happened on Labor Day 2005. We were invited to this beach party. The only fun thing to do at this particular beach party was to play volleyball. My level of annoyance with Earl had reached a fever pitch. I found myself picking him apart for every little thing. I watched him try to spike the ball and all I could think about is how he sucks at net sports.

Take tennis. He hits the ball without turning his body or moving his feet, and all I can do is stand there and watch it, and think of how it's an analogy for his whole life. I scream at him in my head, "Anticipate the ball! Follow through! MOVE YOUR FEET!"

Now here he was playing volleyball. Different net, different ball, but he's still sucking and I'm still picking at him. His pinkness is turning lobster red in the heat of the sun. He tries to dig, misses the ball, and hurts his hand. And in his sort of nonemotional guy way, he says,

"Oh, I hurt my hand. Be right back."

Unwilling to let that spoil my fun, I kept playing while he

went to put some ice on it and sit down under our tent. The game ended and I went to check on him.

"Hey, hon, are you all right?"

The ice is melting, and he's limply holding it to his hand and says, "It hurts, it really hurts."

"Okay, okay."

"I think I might pass out."

"Okay, well, why don't we . . ."

Then he lowers his head down and he draws this death breath . . . hhhhhhmmmmm . . . a deep, rattling inhale, and then just goes limp, stiff limp, and he's gone. *He's just gone.* I picked his head up and kissed him. Nothing.

Then I remember something my father told me. I had watched him revive a man who was having a heart attack by biting his finger. I asked him why he did that and he said, **"When the body is in shock, it will recover if you redirect the pain."**

Redirect the pain.

So I held my fiancé's face in my hand. And I slapped him.

"Where are you, baby?" I pleaded.

Then I could hear my mother's voice ringing through my head:

"He will never change for you—all men leave!"

I pulled my arm back and slapped him again. Harder.

"You promised me you wouldn't leave, Earl!"

His head flops back and his eyes roll into the back of his head.

My mind was racing. Was he dying? Because we had made an agreement that I would die first. If he was going to die today, he should have told me, so I could have killed myself yesterday, and then he could die today. "Earl! Come back!" Nothing. I look up and shout,

"HELP! EARL'S UNCONSCIOUS! HELP!"

I see all these guys, browns and olives with rippling six-packs, throwing horseshoes and flirting with girls, and no one comes to our aid, and I know that if it had been someone else who needed help, sweet, pink Earl would have been the first one on the scene to help, no matter what. I once watched him jump into a swimming pool fully clothed because some drunk stranger had tripped and fallen in. I've seen him break up vicious dog fights, and he voluntarily rubs my legs until I fall asleep when I'm stressed.

I realized that for all those guys up and down that beach, Earl was the only one I wanted anything to do with. Here was my favorite person in the whole world, my best friend, my partner in crime, the only person I truly love or even really like, unconscious in front of me. *I do not want to do this life without him.*

Redirect the pain. I slapped him a third time as hard as I could . . . the next thing I was going to do was lay him down and give him CPR . . . and then his head swiveled to life on its own and he blinked open his lakelike blues. Tears of relief pooled in my eyes. "Baby, you scared the shit out of me."

"I think I passed out," he muttered.

"Uh, yeah, you passed out."

Earl's hand really hurt, but he was fine. The X-rays showed nothing and he wore a splint on his finger for a couple weeks. He just passed out because when it comes to pain, he's a pussy.

Earl barely remembers the incident, but when we got

home that night after the beach party, I was different. For those forty-five seconds while he was gone, my life was meaningless without him and I was alone in the world. I now knew for certain I wouldn't trade him for anybody. Suddenly, all the little problems we have and all the little things he does that bother me didn't matter to me at all.

After nearly five years of being together, in that moment, on that beach, in my heart, I became his wife.

A Wedding in Vegas

Earl and I continued to enjoy our peaceful cohabitation much to the chagrin of our parents. Then finally, one Saturday in February, Earl and I woke up and started kidding around about it being a nice day for an elopement. We teased about how great it would be all day long, until by 6 P.M. we were dead serious. We tried to get a flight to Vegas that night, but they were all booked. The wind let out of our sails, we decided it was time to set a date—a date very soon. A month later, we did fly to Vegas, with sixteen friends from all over the country and a live webcast for everyone else. We wrote our own vows and giggled our way through them. The rumor mill was fascinating; I later found out that several people were speculating that I might be pregnant. Nope, just a deep desire to take the big plunge Earl and Cindy style.

At a dinner party before our wedding, Earl admitted that he was mostly doing it to please me, and that was enough motivation for him. But now he says that for him, watching me walk down that aisle, standing up and making that promise, exchanging rings, and sharing that first kiss as husband and wife linked his soul to mine. The same way I hooked into him while he was passed out on that beach. From the moment we left our neon chapel, he was changed. Just as I had been that day on the beach. A softness crept into his heart and he could not stop calling me *his wife*. "You are my wife. This is my wife. Hello, wife." Again and again he says it with a tenderness, a pride, and an intention that stretches into forever and stills my heart. In that chapel, just down the hall from that casino, in the most lawless state in the union, he became my husband.

We make each other fearless, we always know that we are a team of two, and we are constantly evolving ourselves and our love.

My Prince Charming is a tall, pink, quiet guy from Minnesota with a shaved head. And I haven't looked at another man since. (Okay, I *look*, but that's it.)

Thanks to The Four Man Plan, I will always know that he stayed to win my hand, and that I chose him over all other men and my stupid Quest. And we are both better people for it.

12. THE 4MPLANNER'S PLANNER

Sample 4MPlanners and all the Mantris Graphs you'll need for four months of successful 4MPlanning.

"Have FUN, dammit!"

—CINDY LU

4MPlanners' Success Stories

When I started hearing from women who were actually doing The Plan, I nearly peed myself. What started out as a personal endeavor is proving useful to other women—lots of other women. I started getting e-mails from all over the country and then all over the world: faraway places like Kenya, Japan, Israel, and Russia. 4MPlanners were revealing themselves in a variety of ages, races, and economic and religious backgrounds. The more girls wrote, the more I got involved. There's nothing more frustrating than listening to your girlfriend tell you she's in love AGAIN and this time it's going to work out even though you know it's not because she simply sucks at love. But there's nothing JUICIER and more delightful than hearing about a woman juggling men with grace, self-awareness, and a forward momentum. Turns out, there is nothing more fun than dishing about The Plan!

This chapter shares the stories of four of my favorite 4MPlanners. These ladies really put The Plan into action and got all sorts of delicious results. Get yourself totally inspired and then bust out the blank Mantris Graphs starting on page 191 and start up your own experiment with The Plan. Be a part of Dating's Evolution.

4MPlanner Stella—The Busy Bee

Stella is an actress and business owner in her twenties. Stella's use of The Plan was creative and fun, just like her. Before doing The Plan, her first and longest relationship had been with a man twenty years her senior. (Daddy?) Since then, none of her relationships had lasted longer than three months.

To Stella, nice guys were wusses and her favorite brand of men were those who underestimated her so she could spend her time proving herself. In the past, Stella had had the knee-jerk reaction of hopping right into the sack, so NOT doing that was going to be a challenge for her. "I'm so used to having sex right away as a way of saying, 'Please like me!'" she confided. But she was starting to feel like that was all men liked her for. After reading The 4MP, Stella suspected that her reckless vagina had been steering the boat and that perhaps a lack of proper communication between her and her hoo-ha had led to some of the negative reactions she received from men. When she took on the challenge of The Plan, she was a little nervous: "It's a bit scary, as it is a new way of looking at things, but I am GAME!"

Her first Quarter Man was Designer Dude, and after their first date, he sent her a box of his gorgeous clothes—even though they hadn't even kissed! Stella was shocked by this generous gesture: "That's never happened!" By her third date with him, a big make-out session on the couch made him a Whole Man.

Stella fretted that she would scare off Designer Dude by falling back into her old pattern of focusing on one man as soon as things got physical. So she busted out The Methods of Collection to get herself a pocketful of Quarters. Stella let The Plan crack her brain so wide open that she even included Red Man—someone she previously would have considered a political nemesis with a major deal-breaking quality.

Following The Two-Date-Minimum with these new Plan Men really helped her shift out of her old snap judgments. "I used to think I could tell if I liked a guy or not in the first two minutes. But knowing that I had to go out with them again, I started to see all of their amazing qualities that I would have otherwise missed!" Everyone has something groovy to offer. Consider each date a treasure hunt—after all, there could be a heart of gold beating under that W pin. New Quarters Pilot Guy and Tall Boy were way more fun than she expected. And Red Man earned a smoldering kiss good night at the end of their third date, which bumped him up to a Whole Man.*

Before doing The Plan, Stella had avoided men who were persistent and kind while simultaneously moaning about how there were no nice guys out there. Oh, the irony. A few weeks in, Stella had developed a good eye for the good guy— but then she had a minor Plan-ic Attack because new Quarter Man, Artist Boy, was treating her *too* well and it made her deeply uncomfortable. "Help!!! He is sooooo nice, I'm freaking out!" Luckily, she realized that "too sweet" did not qualify him for The Ickies and she persevered.

---

*If every Red State girl married a Blue State boy and every Blue State girl would marry a Red State boy, then they would make a nation full of purple babies. Everyone would get along, and WE CAN SAVE THE WORLD!

For their fifth date, Designer Dude made Stella baked ziti without meat to honor her vegetarianism. Very nice! And for their next date, he suggested that she "bring her toothbrush." But Stella was using The Wait for Sex Index, and by her measurements, she wasn't ready to go there with him just yet and told him so. He stamped and pouted for a bit, but Stella held her ground. So instead, he suggested a couples massage and a movie. A much better sixth date!

Successfully keeping Designer Dude at Whole Man level got Stella very excited. It *is* exciting when you realize that without sex, a man will actually find other ways to spend time with you. What they suggest as alternate activities tells you a lot more about what a potential relationship would be like with them than a half hour of grunting in the dark.*

After four months on The Plan, Stella's career got very demanding and keeping a full Mantris Graph was more than she could handle. So she decided to put the graph and her extraneous Plan Men on hold. Hey, don't let The Plan make you crazy. Take time off when you need it. The Plan does not require any minimum time allotment or weekly dating quota, so just spend whatever time you want to spend on it. End your semester whenever you see fit; the 3½ man is not the only successful outcome.

---

*The fact is, once you get into a relationship, even if you have sex seven days a week, even if you have it for a whole hour, that's only 4.1666 percent of your day. So to really know what it would be like to marry a guy, it's a good idea to explore what that other 95.8334 percent of the time with him might be like.

Stella took the tools she learned and stuck them in her man-bag, never to be forgotten. Now she's moved on to a Graphless Plan. She continues dating without trying to keep a full docket, while still employing the important Principles of The Plan. Do your life right and keep The Plan handy.

"The 4MPlan has helped me learn how to allow a relationship to unfold naturally and to respect myself and my body enough to not have to jump into bed. Having a variety of men in my life made it so I didn't hyperfocus on someone who may or may not be a match for me. I can stand in my power and I get to decide. I am no longer losing who I am because I'm trying to morph into what I think any one particular guy wants me to be.

"I am still learning and will probably take out the graph again soon! It is a great tool! But even better than The Mantris Graph are the lessons that are learned from throwing yourself into this new way of looking at and experiencing dating. I have not found my 3½ man yet, but I am getting closer and the men that are coming to me are showing me how much I am changing. I promise that if you really do it you will reap amazing benefits!"

—Stella

Stella's Mantris Graph

4MPlanner Chelsea—The Teacher's Pet

Chelsea is in her thirties and a very successful career girl. She became my most diligent 4MPlanner and the first to input her Plan Men into her Mantris Graph using Excel! She blogged me weekly, and every Monday morning I would wake up early and sit at my computer with a cup of tea, anxious to read the juicy details. I loved my breakfasts with Chelsea.

Chelsea came to The Plan as an overgiving serial monogamist with a suspicious streak inherited from her dear mama. "My never-married status proves that this tack was not working for me," she confided. More than anything, Chelsea needed to learn to receive and trust.

In her first week on The Plan, she had two dates with two new men. She hadn't done that in over a decade! Why do we wait so long? The Plan gives the 4MPlanner a hot poker in the butt back into what can be the very fun world of dating. It's ours for the taking!

While Chelsea was getting to know her Quarter Men, Anthony, an Ex Reflex, resurfaced and took over the coveted 2¼ position.*

When Quarter Man Evan picked Chelsea up for their first date, he was dressed nicely and smelled great. He

---

*Remember, The Plan is a perfect time to explore your pool of unresolved Exes. It's a chance to get closure or explore why things didn't work out. Or sometimes the Ex Reflex is just about some really hot rolls in the hay while you hold other Plan Men at bay. Feel free to take the time to research your history in order to improve your future. Meanwhile, don't get sucked back into the vortex—keep that Mantris Graph cooking!

brought her a little gift and took her to dinner and a comedy show. She nearly busted a gasket from all the giving he was lavishing upon her, but she let it happen. Evan's thoughtfulness made a real impression on Chelsea, who realized she had been dating freeloaders for far too long. She had gotten accustomed to paying on dates so she wouldn't feel obligated to sleep with them.* Instead, it was just making it easy for men to use her. The kindness and willingness that Evan displayed made her question why she had spent so long pining over the emotionally unavailable Anthony. Slowly but surely, she was unsucking at love.

Before long, Chelsea had collected a few other Quarter and Half Men who rivaled Evan's great planning, generosity, and excellent taste. Her newfound fabulousness really made her a hot ticket. "I had clearly opened myself up to receiving—instead of just giving all the time (and then bitching about it) as I had in the past," she told me. It's amazing what can happen when you trade in your Eau de Desperate for a spritz of Parfum de La Plan.

She eventually Chucked Out Ex Anthony to promote Evan to her Two and a Quarter during an intensely romantic weekend together. Chelsea thought that all that was left to

---

*Somewhere along the line, women have started believing that a man paying for dates means that you owe him some sort of sexual payment. HELL NO! Take the time to be gorgeous and charming and make the most of your date's positive attributes and know that your company is pleasure enough. Most important, embrace the joy of receiving! Men LOVE to see that a woman is pleased by their efforts. Let someone do something nice for you and know that you are worth it.

do was wait for him to ask for a monogamous relationship and carefully employed The Talk Paradox. While she waited, she patiently dated her other Plan Men.

Then, late one night, she got a surprising and devastating phone call. Evan Dropped Out, stating the I'm-just-not-that-into-you Defense. LAME. And for Chelsea—ouch! Getting dumped suddenly is very upsetting whether you are doing The Plan or not. A marathon performance of The "What Went Wrong?" Show played in Chelsea's head. "That night I was only able to sleep a few hours before waking up in complete darkness, with Evan on my mind and pressure weighing on my heart," she said. She could have speculated endlessly about what made him back away, of course, but that would have been a colossal waste of her time.

Instead, she decided to assume that he was telling his absolute truth, as we are instructed to do with all Plan Men until otherwise proven. As painful as it was, Chelsea honored his word, released him graciously, and moved on. Evan was a great example of why WILLING becomes such a crucial criterion when looking for a man.* By being classy in response to his Dropping Out, Chelsea left the door open for Evan to return later, if she was still available. (Which, by the way, months later, he did try to, but by then she was SO OVER him.) That's the chance a man takes when he drops out. Later, when he is still single, but old and crusty, he will pine

---

*A healthy relationship takes two willing participants. Anything less than that is a treadmill of misplaced hope that leads to lots of quiet suffering and late-night chocolate eating.

away for you, the one that got away. You will be his Chuck, and that is all the revenge you will ever need.

Chelsea was the Queen of Recovery and managed to remain open and loving and on the 4MP. She still had her other Plan Men, after all, and by aggressively employing The Yes Factor and the power of the Internet Connection, she began dating more Plan Men, promoting some and collecting others. She received a Tiffany necklace from the Good Doctor and worked on her trust issues with Rocco. She had fun sex with frisky young Leo and taught the Drill Sergeant how to use chopsticks. When I asked her how she was feeling about Evan, she said, "I'm sorry, Evan who?"

Chelsea soon realized that she wanted to feel something deeper during sex than she had in the past. So she demoted Leo to a Whole Man and swore off casual sex. She became more aware that SHE needed to be ready to take a relationship to that level, and that her Slide Rule of Intimacy had shifted a few notches. Yes, when you stop sacrificing your vagina as your first line of attack, even a kiss can become intimate and precious.

Sexually tamed, Chelsea became bold and daring in other areas of her life and actually made a trip to Hawaii *alone,* where she met a man while dancing and another on a hike and another on the plane home. She was on fire and having to squeeze men out left and right!

Then, upon her return, she met Speed Racer—a passionate and funny teddy bear of a man. They made plans to meet and he was so very not her type. But Chemistry Shmemistry, when he asked to take her out for dinner on her birthday, which is, oddly enough, Valentine's Day, she happily accepted. "Speed Racer totally outdid EVERY MAN that evening!" she recalled. The next morning, she sent Speed Racer a thank-you card for the best birthday she'd ever had. "Now that I don't use blow jobs as praise, I'm getting much better at using my words!"

At the end of her fourth date with Speed Racer, Chelsea kissed him and a little more, and he officially became a Whole Man. And then he asked her if they could see each other exclusively! But she was having so much fun on The Plan, she told him she would have to think about it. A week later, however, she agreed to be monogamous with him, cordially released her other Plan Men, took her profile off Yahoo personals, and then settled into the arms of her 3½ Man.

Now it's time for her to breathe, relax, and enjoy. She is in love with herself and now life will follow. Yay, Chelsea!

> "Six months of following The Four Man Plan significantly changed the way I dated and seriously upgraded the caliber of men I attracted. I behaved lighter on dates; I had so much fun, and (thanks to The Wait for Sex Index) I got to know each Plan Man so much more authentically than I had in the past. In the end, it all led me to my handsome and affectionate 3½ Man! I can totally be myself with Speed Racer. He tells me that he's different with me than he's been with any other woman ever, and he makes me feel special. And that's what I've always wanted!"
>
> —Chelsea

Chelsea's Mantris Graph

4MPlanner Ellie—The Phoenix

Ellie is a forty-year-old, newly single mom with two young kids. If you think you've been challenged in your love life, get a load of Ellie. After fifteen years of marriage and raising two children together, her husband finally admitted to her that he was attracted to men—in other words, her husband was gay. KABOOM! Yeah, it actually happens. Ellie was devastated and began to question everything about herself. How did this happen? Did she drive him to it? What did it mean about her, as a woman? After months of reeling from the shock and wondering if she would ever be able to embark on another relationship with a man, she found The Four Man Plan.

Ellie incubated the idea of trying The 4MP for many weeks. Then she started slowly, and with one of my favorite sources for a Plan Man, a mutual friend set up Joe. After a lovely first lunch date, but no postdate call from him, she followed The Two-Date Minimum and invited him to a show a week later. And with that, a sexually charged second date resulted in some much-needed hanky-panky, and Joe became a Whole Man.

But her divorce was very fresh, and Ellie knew that her love life needed to be about her healing and not Joe, Joe, Joe, Joe. So she lined up lunch dates with two Quarter Men in order to keep her relationship with Joe in balance.

On their third date, she and Joe had wildly hot sex. *Hurrah!* Remember that there are no "rules" as to when you should make a man your 2¼. It's whatever feels right for you, and that can change based on where you are in The Plan, your life, or the man you are with. Given the way her marriage had ended, it was time for Ellie to kick up her heels.

But since she was committed to doing The Plan, she had to make sure to Halve Joe and let him know she was dating other men before the end of the third-date deadline. Technically, she should have done it when he became a Whole Man, but she let Lu's Pendulum swing the other way and got back on track. "Joe and I discussed the fact that we are going to date others but only sleep with each other. That conversation went much smoother than I expected," she told me.*

Soon Ellie really had the hang of The Plan and a nearly full Graph. She had terrific chemistry on her first date with Batman and was hot to trot. But Joe was her 2¼, and with a full understanding of The Rule of Chuck, Ellie stopped and thought about it before jumping into bed with someone new. She found that simply knowing she was desirable was way more valuable than actually having sex with Batman. Which she was grateful for, since he was eventually discarded for being more like The Penguin and giving her The Ickies. Can you imagine what a bummer it would have been if she had let him into her Batcave and had to Chuck Out Joe, whom she really liked? Phew! Close call, Super 4MPlanner!

---

*It always surprises my 4MPlanners to find that Plan Men are not bothered by the fact that they are dating other men, but instead relieved and/or intrigued. It may bug them at first and they may even step away for a moment. But it also makes them think about whether or not you are worth fighting for. And when they make that decision, men with real potential will most likely wander back into your Mantris or take the plunge and ask to become your 3½ Man.

But things with Joe were not entirely smooth sailing, and soon Ellie had a Plan-ic Attack because Joe could go as long as a week or more without talking to her. He, too, was divorced with kids, and when the holidays rolled around, family activities kept him away. Ellie started doubting herself and creating false scenarios. This is the kind of mental crap that clutters a gal's mind and eats up her energy. We women love to create a mix tape of our Top 10 Insecurities and round it out with a few Oldies But Goodies Fantasies and play them on a loop in our head. Luckily, The 4MP pushed pause on that playback for Ellie when things took another interesting turn.

Ellie had been corresponding with a few Quarter Men online, and to her surprise, she found herself becoming more intrigued by Slow Man, even though they hadn't met yet. The Internet Connection recommends speaking to and meeting a well-chosen Plan Man found online before getting too excited by letters on a screen, which she did. Slow Man served as a distraction that soon paid off. When Ellie finally got a message from Joe saying that he would call her when he returned from his vacation, her response was "I am fine waiting for him to call me—now that Slow Man is in the picture!"

Soon after, Ellie's best friend's husband had a major stroke and Ellie was on board to help them through. It would be impossible for her to try to keep her Mantris full, but she continued with her already established Plan Men. A natural-born giver, maybe too much so at times, Ellie used The Plan to make sure that she made a little time for herself and for fun while she nurtured her friends. Slow Man offered his support by e-mailing several Web sites that he had found on strokes in hopes that this would help Ellie help her friend. "That was better than bringing me a dozen red roses!" And he really helped take her mind off things one night by the fireplace when he came over and they kissed for two hours! Slow Man became a Whole Man—and she renamed him Favorite Man to boot!

Ellie was still dating Favorite Man when Joe came back into the picture. "I feel a little guilty about dating Joe while I am getting closer emotionally with Favorite Man," she said. *

Ellie didn't realize it at the time, but The Wait for Sex Index and The Rule of Chuck were working perfectly for her! By not having sex with Favorite Man, other forms of intimacy were given a chance to develop. And at the same time, she had not jeopardized a possible future relationship with Joe. Joe was close to her physically, while Favorite Man was supporting her emotionally. Ellie's needs were being met without her having to take on the task of a full-time relationship at a time when she wasn't ready for one. Everyone wins!

Eventually, hectic schedules and different lifestyles caused Favorite Man to Drop Out. It was bittersweet but very sane. He had helped her through a difficult time and she was still happily dating others. "We were very good to each other. I learned a lot from Favorite Man and our time together, so I was fine with it ending."

---

*When you're on The Plan, guilt is pointless. It's just a way of squirming out and limiting yourself. All parties involved are grown-ups; the men have been told the truth and are doing what they want. Let The Disney Theorem work its magic guilt-free!

As she moved into the throes of her divorce settlement, she decided to take time off from The Plan until she was in a place where she was really ready to get serious with someone.

The 4MP has opened the door for a whole new future for Ellie—she got her ducks in a row, her socks knocked off, and her heart sewn up. She is now successfully single and Joe waits patiently in the wings. . . .

"Working The Four Man Plan, I have learned to be more compassionate and patient with myself and men. Most importantly, I regained the self-confidence I lost while being in a marriage with a homosexual man. I get it now, and I don't need a bunch of sex to prove to me what I already know—I am desirable, I am beautiful inside and out, I am worthy, and I am a great catch!"

—Ellie

Ellie's Mantris Graph

4MPlanner Georgia—The Grande Dame

Georgia is in her late fifties and has been married twice. Her first marriage lasted fourteen years and ended in a painful divorce; the second time, she was happily married for seventeen years until her husband died suddenly in 2003. Georgia is also a grandmother who keeps physically active. She is a salsa-dancing fool and even sent me an adorable picture of her in a wet suit with her surfboard at the beach!

All in all, Georgia has been married more years than she's been single. "Those of us who have been married a long time and suddenly find ourselves dating are maybe even more clueless than girls just starting out," she explained. As far as marriage goes, Georgia could probably teach the rest of us a few tricks, but as a single gal, she sucked at love. The Four Man Plan gave her the gumption to get back out there after years of being out of circulation.

As soon as she started The Plan, Georgia dropped the arm-length Expectation List she had developed based on her loving husband, and to her surprise, she collected two Quarter Men in less than twenty-four hours! She went to a concert and got her first business card. Then she struck up a nice conversation with someone at the market and got her second e-mail address. "I was like a butterfly gathering nectar from flower to flower," she giggled.

Georgia also had a salsa dancing 2¼ man tucked away who was much younger and who was, as she put it, an "in-the-meantime relationship." She had been trying in vain to make it into more than that, but now that she had the 4MP, she realized she could still enjoy her young buck while being open to something serious. So she let him know she was dating. This was a perfect use of the 2¼—it gave her elusive lover a choice to either step up their relationship or keep things the same while she explored her options.

Georgia was reading along happily when she came across, *gulp,* The Chick's Chick Angle. She realized that by going after The Ineligible, a friend's man, she had been a Dick's Chick. Boooo. "I apologized to my friend and we cried. It was humbling. The Plan relieved me of having to compete for another woman's man and gave me rules of how to play the game with integrity, and that is my favorite part."

Georgia followed The Yes Factor and The Two-Date Minimum with a number of Quarter Men, and then, for the first time ever, started looking online for a few more to fill her Graph. Jay was the second man she went out with from Match.com. "We just clicked. Honestly, I think we fell in love the moment we saw each other," she told me. Still, she knew that they needed to take it slow enough to figure out if what they felt for each other was real, so she continued seeing other Quarter Men. "The Plan allowed me to feel free and at ease, not needy. It made all the difference."*

---

*Getting really excited about someone can often cause us to lunge at them and scare them away. Often we create a fantasy that is unreasonable based on the very few encounters we have. Guys find this unbelievably ooky. And even if you don't share your weird little fantasies with them, it's like spraying yourself with man-repellent. They can sense it and it blocks them from coming toward you, because they don't want to be saddled with unreasonable expectations. Keeping things in perspective and giving them the appropriate percentage of your attention helps to keep them from running away from something with real potential.

By the end of her second month, the 4MP had worked so well that Georgia ended it and started seeing Jay exclusively. He'd known all along that she was dating, and it didn't take long before he asked her to give them a chance by just seeing each other. So she told her 2¼ Man that she had met someone she really liked and that she would be moving on. He was sad and so was she, but he understood. Jay became her 3½ Man.

Three months later, I heard from Georgia again: "Last weekend Jay and I got engaged. I'm very, very happy!" she wrote. Ah, the Distribution of Love Gods have shined favorably upon her. Georgia became my very first engaged 4MPlanner! She has been successfully married before and she knows what she is looking for. "Jay is honest, loving, and willing (willing is definitely crucial!) and so much more: generous, fun, handsome, gentle, talented, gorgeous, and on and on. Our lives fit nicely . . . it's really good. He's got the same talents that I've always been attracted to, but he's of mixed ethnicity and that's something new for me and very, very attractive. And I'll confess he thinks I'm hot too!"

Congratulations, Georgia! May your years with Jay be glorious and joyful.

Gutsy Georgia made it look easy. It's never too late to master the big waves of The Plan. Cowabunga, Grandma!

Georgia's Mantris Graph

"The Four Man Plan is brilliant. It turned out to be the most perfect way to ease out of the old life and find the new one. I gave everyone a chance and I had several possibilities working, so I wasn't needy. I was happy and having a great time dating. In the end, romance prevailed!

"So many, many thanks for your fun, funny, and most effective wisdom. I hope all your other 4MPlanners can enjoy the process as much as I did. Thanks again. It really works!"
—Georgia

How to Use the Blank Mantris

	Plan Man	Value	▲ or ▼	Notes
1.	ROMEO	2 1/4	NEW	EX REFLEX
2.	NICK	1/4	NEW	MIME
3.	MALAKA HIKI HI	1	↑	SAID HE LOVES ME
4.	MARLBORO MAN	1/2	↑	SHOOK MALAKA'S HAND
5.				
6.				
7.				
8.				
9.				
10.				

The Four Man Plan

Week # ____

	Plan Man	Value	▲ or ▼	Notes
1.				
2.				
3.				
4.				
5.				
6.				
7.				
8.				
9.				
10.				

The Four Man Plan

Week # _____

	Plan Man	Value	▲ or ▼	Notes
1.	_____	____	____	_____
2.	_____	____	____	_____
3.	_____	____	____	_____
4.	_____	____	____	_____
5.	_____	____	____	_____
6.	_____	____	____	_____
7.	_____	____	____	_____
8.	_____	____	____	_____
9.	_____	____	____	_____
10.	_____	____	____	_____

The Four Man Plan

Week # ____

Plan Man	Value	▲ or ▼	Notes
1. _____	_____	_____	_____
2. _____	_____	_____	_____
3. _____	_____	_____	_____
4. _____	_____	_____	_____
5. _____	_____	_____	_____
6. _____	_____	_____	_____
7. _____	_____	_____	_____
8. _____	_____	_____	_____
9. _____	_____	_____	_____
10. _____	_____	_____	_____

The Four Man Plan

Week # ____

	Plan Man	Value	▲ or ▼	Notes
1.	_____	_____	_____	_____
2.	_____	_____	_____	_____
3.	_____	_____	_____	_____
4.	_____	_____	_____	_____
5.	_____	_____	_____	_____
6.	_____	_____	_____	_____
7.	_____	_____	_____	_____
8.	_____	_____	_____	_____
9.	_____	_____	_____	_____
10.	_____	_____	_____	_____

The Four Man Plan

Week # ____

Plan Man	Value	▲ or ▼	Notes
1. _____	_____	_____	_____
2. _____	_____	_____	_____
3. _____	_____	_____	_____
4. _____	_____	_____	_____
5. _____	_____	_____	_____
6. _____	_____	_____	_____
7. _____	_____	_____	_____
8. _____	_____	_____	_____
9. _____	_____	_____	_____
10. _____	_____	_____	_____

The Four Man Plan

Week # ____

	Plan Man	Value	▲ or ▼	Notes
1.	_____	_____	_____	_____
2.	_____	_____	_____	_____
3.	_____	_____	_____	_____
4.	_____	_____	_____	_____
5.	_____	_____	_____	_____
6.	_____	_____	_____	_____
7.	_____	_____	_____	_____
8.	_____	_____	_____	_____
9.	_____	_____	_____	_____
10.	_____	_____	_____	_____

The Four Man Plan

Week # _____

Plan Man	Value	▲ or ▼	Notes
1. _____	_____	_____	_____
2. _____	_____	_____	_____
3. _____	_____	_____	_____
4. _____	_____	_____	_____
5. _____	_____	_____	_____
6. _____	_____	_____	_____
7. _____	_____	_____	_____
8. _____	_____	_____	_____
9. _____	_____	_____	_____
10. _____	_____	_____	_____

The Four Man Plan

Week # ____

Plan Man	Value	▲ or ▼	Notes
1.			
2.			
3.			
4.			
5.			
6.			
7.			
8.			
9.			
10.			

The Four Man Plan

Week # ____

Plan Man	Value	▲ or ▼	Notes
1. _____	____	____	_____
2. _____	____	____	_____
3. _____	____	____	_____
4. _____	____	____	_____
5. _____	____	____	_____
6. _____	____	____	_____
7. _____	____	____	_____
8. _____	____	____	_____
9. _____	____	____	_____
10. _____	____	____	_____

The Four Man Plan

Week # ____

Plan Man	Value	▲ or ▼	Notes
1.			
2.			
3.			
4.			
5.			
6.			
7.			
8.			
9.			
10.			

The Four Man Plan

Week # ____

Plan Man	Value	▲ or ▼	Notes
1. _____	_____	_____	_____
2. _____	_____	_____	_____
3. _____	_____	_____	_____
4. _____	_____	_____	_____
5. _____	_____	_____	_____
6. _____	_____	_____	_____
7. _____	_____	_____	_____
8. _____	_____	_____	_____
9. _____	_____	_____	_____
10. _____	_____	_____	_____

The Four Man Plan

Week # ____

Plan Man	Value	▲ or ▼	Notes
1. _____	_____	_____	_____
2. _____	_____	_____	_____
3. _____	_____	_____	_____
4. _____	_____	_____	_____
5. _____	_____	_____	_____
6. _____	_____	_____	_____
7. _____	_____	_____	_____
8. _____	_____	_____	_____
9. _____	_____	_____	_____
10. _____	_____	_____	_____

The Four Man Plan

Week # ____

	Plan Man	Value	▲ or ▼	Notes
1.	_____	_____	_____	_____
2.	_____	_____	_____	_____
3.	_____	_____	_____	_____
4.	_____	_____	_____	_____
5.	_____	_____	_____	_____
6.	_____	_____	_____	_____
7.	_____	_____	_____	_____
8.	_____	_____	_____	_____
9.	_____	_____	_____	_____
10.	_____	_____	_____	_____

The Four Man Plan

Week # ____

Plan Man	Value	▲ or ▼	Notes
1. _____	____	____	_____
2. _____	____	____	_____
3. _____	____	____	_____
4. _____	____	____	_____
5. _____	____	____	_____
6. _____	____	____	_____
7. _____	____	____	_____
8. _____	____	____	_____
9. _____	____	____	_____
10. _____	____	____	_____

In Sum

I love The Plan. Not just because I designed it, not because it brought me Earl. I love it because it has brought me closer to myself. All my dramas and traumas and running in circles with men were really just an elaborate way of avoiding figuring myself out.

My ultimate wish for any girl who does The Plan is that she end her run on the gerbil wheel of love. Not only will she no longer suck at love, a 4MPlanner will have gained a deeper understanding about how much power she has through how she perceives men and relationships. She will spend her life being her absolute best self and live in a world full of love that she created.

This society, where people can survive alone, without teamwork, without a partner, has turned love into a luxury item. An accessory that we think we have infinite choice over and shouldn't settle for anything less than perfection. But even though we can go on breathing without love, you aren't truly living without it. Deep down we know that love is essential and perfection isn't possible.

I created a structure for love because it is within a structure that we learn to improve. Structure creates limitations, and limitations are the inspiration of creativity and brilliance. It makes room for both the intuitive (keep your eye on the ball) and the counterintuitive (jump and the net will appear).

A few of my 4MPlanners have asked after doing The Plan for several weeks, "Where have all these great guys been this whole time?" Well, these may be the exact same men that treat some women badly or just use them for sex. We cannot discount the possibility that they, too, have been shopping for marriage material and have been disappointed by their selection. Women must understand that we set the water level that men learn to swim in. When they find a woman of quality and depth, they will enjoy rising to the challenge of being her equal and so much more.

The net that has appeared to catch me is a beautiful community of women, each of us pulling the other up with whatever we have to give. I have received more treasures from my girlfriends and 4MPlanners than all the imaginary bounty I was chasing after by seeking the approval of men.

There is always the wistful notion that is passed around,

"If only the world were run by women . . ."

If we add up all the wasted time and energy women spend flailing and wailing over men and channel it toward who we really are, then that notion can be a reality. It's our turn to give running the world a try, don't you think?

Within this latest edition of The Plan, I've considered many wonderful dilemmas and insights presented to me by my 4MPlanners and added them to my own. The Four Man Plan has become as intricate and multidimensional as a woman's heart, and that makes me love it even more.

CINDY – Y
+ E(2)ARL(2)
= Cinderella!

The 4MPlanner's Credo

1. Always be yourself.
2. Always tell the truth when asked a direct question.
3. Be honest, loving, and willing and those attributes will be returned to you.
4. Protect other women and their relationships.
5. Believe that good men are everywhere and there are enough to go around.
6. Believe that love can be practiced and enjoyed even when you are not "in love."
7. Believe that dividing your expectations multiplies your chances at love.
8. Believe that love is earned and not found.
9. Believe that your company and attention are gift enough.
10. Believe in the sacredness of your vagina.
11. Have FUN, dammit!

Acknowledgments

My most heartfelt thanks to:

My trusted manager, Kim Matuka.

David Vigliano, Kirsten Neuhaus, and the fantastic team at Vigliano and Associates; and Aaron Shure and Dan Simon for the kismet introduction.

Ann Campbell, Laura Lee Mattingly, and everyone at Broadway Books for their faith and enthusiasm.

Jen Cleary for her tireless work and beautiful and funny graphics, artwork, and photos.

Rizwan Kassim, Math and Science Stud.

Artists David Milano and Jason Hill.

My mentors, advisors, and many, many therapists, including but not limited to: Paul Linke, Rita Navroth, Donna Bloom, Brenda Williams, and Bill Burns.

All of my fabulous girlfriends and 4MPlanners for advice and love exchanged, especially: Shari Albert, Ellen Bartell, Lacey Brooks, Glenna Citron, Marylee Fairbanks, Michelle Latham, Käthe Mazur, Stacy Solodkin, and Lucy Yeh.

The Men who have been a part of my life. Learning from you all has been an amazing gift.

My mom and dad. My dear big sister, An-Chi Campbell.

Master Hua-Ching Ni.

Most of all, to my husband, Earl Martin, for helping me find my voice and letting me share our story.

Illustration Credits

Four Man Plan men on cover and title page: Jason Hill
Line drawing of Albert Einstein: David Milano
Line drawings and figures by Jen Cleary, Cindy Lu
Stick Figure of Cindy Lu: Jen Cleary
4MPlanners Mantris Graphs: Ellen Bartell, Lacey Brooks,
Glenna Citron, Stacy Solodkin, and Lucy Yeh
Cover concept by: Cindy Lu

About the Author

A professional actress for over eighteen years, Cindy Lu has performed in theaters across the country and in dozens of television shows, films, and commercials. *The Four Man Plan* began as a one-woman show in Los Angeles. Between dates and acting gigs, she spent time as a waitress, a bartender, a personal assistant, and an energy healer.

Cindy Lu lives in Culver City, California, with her husband, Earl, and their three dogs. For more information about Cindy Lu and *The Four Man Plan,* visit www.thefourmanplan.com.